Englisch für kaufmännische Berufe

Lehrerhandbuch
Fachkurs Industrie

von
Gerald Arnold
Dieter Jeckel
Arthur George Tompkins

Ernst Klett Verlag
Stuttgart München Düsseldorf Leipzig

Englisch für kaufmännische Berufe
Lehrerhandbuch
Fachkurs Industrie

von
Gerald Arnold
Dieter Jeckel
Arthur George Tompkins

Dieses Werk folgt der reformierten
Rechtschreibung und Zeichensetzung.

Gedruckt auf Recyclingpapier, hergestellt
aus 100% Altpapier.

1. Auflage   1 4 3 2 1 | 2000 1999 98 97

Alle Drucke dieser Auflage können im Unterricht nebeneinander
benutzt werden. Die letzte Zahl bezeichnet das Jahr dieses Druckes.

© Ernst Klett Verlag GmbH, Stuttgart 1997.
Alle Rechte vorbehalten.

Redaktion: Volker Wendland

Druck: Druckhaus Götz GmbH, Ludwigsburg
Printed in Germany.

ISBN 3-12-808410-6

Contents

Introduction 4

Abbreviations and symbols 5

Unit 1 The trainee from Kenya 7

Unit 2 Production 13

Unit 3 Purchasing and storekeeping 19

Unit 4 Marketing 24

Unit 5 Complaints and adjustments 31

Unit 6 Modes of payment 37

Unit 7 Transport 43

Unit 8 Business and jobs in Europe 52

Photocopiable grammar exercises 59

Commercial Correspondence (Prüfungsaufgaben): Key 71

Photocopiable forms 77

Glossary of business terms 83

Introduction

Organization of the Student's Book

The Student's Book consists of 8 Units, each dealing with a different topic. The individual Units are in turn divided into five parts (A, B, C, D, E), reflecting separate aspects of the principal topic. For the sake of flexibility, the Units are not connected with one another; a Unit may be left out or used in a different order from that suggested in the book.

In the appendix to the Student's Book, there are *Files* for role play exercises, a brief *Grammar Survey*, examination exercises in *Commercial Correspondence*, the *Tapescripts* and an alphabetical *Vocabulary*.

Skills

All four skills are trained intensively, although precedence is given to speaking and writing activities. In all tasks and exercises with the heading "Phone calls", listening comprehension and telephoning are practised (generally with the help of a cassette). The listening comprehension exercises are always set up in two phases:
1. Listening for the gist of the text
2. Listening for details

A variety of different text types (e.g. business letters, faxes, advertising texts, product information, newspaper articles) has been chosen to improve the student's reading comprehension.

Role plays

Role plays are used in all Units. These are intended to place the students in everyday situations in business life, all taking place in an industrial context. Some of the role plays are guided, whereas others may be freely worked out by the students. Especially in the case of free role plays, the students should be allowed some time for preparation (e.g. for looking up vocabulary) to make the dialogues as realistic as possible.

Grammar

Please note that the *Grammar Survey* is primarily intended to offer the students immediate help in cases of uncertainty, e.g. when deciding on the right tense in a particular situation. The survey is not intended to replace a grammar book.

Commercial correspondence (Test exercises)

Test exercises on *Enquiry, Quotation, Order, Complaint*, and *Reminder* are provided in the appendix to the Student's Book.

Tapescripts

The *Tapescripts* for all exercises marked with the cassette symbol are also included in the appendix to the Student's Book.

Vocabulary

The alphabetical *Vocabulary* concludes the Student's Book. The list is accompanied by phonetic transcriptions and by the page numbers showing where the words can be found in the text.

Organization of the Teacher's Book

I. Contents, Targets, Methodology, Key

The first part of the Teacher's Book is organized in the same order as the Student's Book, starting with a rough summary of the *Contents and Targets* of the respective Unit, followed by advice on *Methodology* and the *Key* to the exercises. Please note that the keys to the free exercises are only suggestions. Background information (*i*) and additional exercises are also given here.

II. Photocopiable grammar exercises (+ keys)

These are optional and can be used according to the requirements of the class.

III. Keys to the test exercises on *Commercial Correspondence*

IV. Photocopiable forms

V. Glossary of business terms

This glossary lists some specific vocabulary which is used in *Industry*.

VI. Incoterms – Decision charts for buyers and sellers

Abbreviations and symbols

S = Student(s)
T = Teacher

CB = Classroom Book

i   Background information

🗝   Key to the exercises

Student's Book: Klett-Nr. 808400
Cassette: Klett-Nr. 808420
Teacher's Book: Klett-Nr. 808410

UNIT 1
The Trainee from Kenya

Contents/Targets:

This unit centres on John Rono, a trainee from Kenya, who finds a training position with the German company H.A.T. in Remscheid.
The unit also shows the different departments of a typical medium-sized company in Germany and some of the business carried out there.

Starter: The S are presented with a reply to John Rono's application.

A: The S learn to introduce themselves and each other, to welcome visitors and to start a first conversation (small talk).

B: The S get acquainted with the various departments of a company and are able to inform others which person is responsible for which tasks/work/sector in the company.

C: The S learn the most important elements and the layout of an English business letter, as well as the difference between a formal and an informal letter.

D: The standard telephone phrases are taught and practice is given in using them.

E: Here, the S learn to work with a more difficult English text and to use a dictionary.

Starter

Methodology

Warm-up:
The T could use either some introductory questions (e.g. Are there any foreign trainees in your company? Where do they come from?) or write some key words on the blackboard (trainee, company, tasks and responsibilities, career prospects) thus eliciting associations from the S and drawing up a mind map.

Key 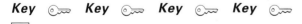 *Key* *Key* *Key*

a
1. F, 2. T, 3. T, 4. F, 5. T

b
He can make himself familiar with the production techniques and the products of the firm and he gets to know the employees in the production department.

c
When a person seeks employment in Germany from outside the EU, the authorities require a visa, and this is normally only granted if the potential employee can prove that a job is waiting for him. The purpose of this is to stop people from coming to Germany, not being able to find a job, and turning to crime.

A
Welcome to H.A.T.

a
Methodology
The T asks two S to play the roles of John and Arnold. Another S or the T can play the part of the staff manager.

Additional questions: What else could you say when you pick someone up at the airport (e.g. Can I help you with your luggage? Would you like to eat/drink something before I take you to the company?)?

b
Methodology
The T asks one of the S (male) to read out the example given, taking another S (female) and introducing her to the class as Sarah. A further S, playing the part of John, makes polite comments, as found in the box on page 10. Then the S playing Sarah could introduce another person from the class to John.

Key *Key* *Key* *Key*

Manfred: This is Sarah. She's from Stockholm and she's been here in the company for three months. Just now, she's working in the sales department.
John: How do you do?
Sarah: Welcome to H.A.T. It's nice to meet you. But I'd like you to meet Birthe. She's been working here for 6 months. At present she's working in the public relations department.
John: I'm pleased to meet you. I'm John, and I'm from Kenya.
Birthe: Hi. I'm sure you'll like the company. We're all friends here. And you know Arnold, don't you?
John: Yes, he met me at the airport and brought me here.

c
Methodology

Before starting the role play, the S should be given some time for preparation, e.g. for studying the phrases on page 11 or for looking up unknown words.

Key 🗝 **Key** 🗝 **Key** 🗝 **Key** 🗝

(Suggestions)

Student A: How long did it take from Nairobi to Düsseldorf?
Student B: Oh, I left Nairobi at 8 am local time and arrived in Düsseldorf at 3 pm.
Student A: Have you been to Germany before?
Student B: No, I've never been to Germany before.
Student A: I hope, you'll like it. What is your country like?
Student B: Oh, it's quite different from Germany, especially the weather.
Student A: Would you like to see our town? I could show you some important places and facilities you should know and where to go shopping.
Student B: Yes, that would be fine. And it's very kind of you to show me around.

Additional exercise: Saying goodbye

Warm-up: What do you say when a foreign visitor is leaving?
The T collects phrases used when saying goodbye and lists them on the blackboard. Phrases can, of course, be formal and informal, depending on the situation. A typical list might be like the one in the following box:

Saying goodbye:	
Formal	**Informal**
We hope you enjoyed your stay with us.	It's been nice having you here.
When do you intend to visit us again?	When are you coming back?
Will we be seeing you at the trade fair next year?	See you again at the trade fair next year.
Please give my regards to Mr/Ms …	Say hello to …
I look forward to seeing you on Tuesday.	See you on Tuesday.
Goodbye!	Bye!/See you!
Goodbye and thank you very much for your invitation.	Bye and thanks for everything.
Goodbye. Have a safe and comfortable flight.	Have a nice flight/trip home.

The T asks the S to find appropriate phrases to say goodbye in different situations:
1. A colleague is leaving the firm. He has been offered a job with better career prospects by another company (Possible phrase: It's a pity that you're leaving, but I/we wish you all the best in your new job.).
2. It's the end of an informal get-together. You'll be seeing the other business partners the following Monday (Possible phrase: Bye. See you on Monday.).
3. A visitor from Manila is going home after a two-week-stay in Germany (Possible phrase: We hope your stay in Germany was interesting and informative for you. We wish you a comfortable and safe flight home.).

d
Methodology

The T could ask the S to find other examples and possible responses.

Key 🗝 **Key** 🗝 **Key** 🗝 **Key** 🗝

(Note: More than one answer is possible.)

1. You're welcome./Not at all.
2. That's all right.
3. Of course!
4. Oh, dear!/I'm sorry to hear that./ Don't worry.
5. That's great!/Really?
6. I'm sorry to hear that.
7. Of course./That's all right.
8. That's great!/Really?
9. Oh, dear!/Really?/I'm sorry to hear that.
10. You're welcome./That's all right./Not at all.

B
Getting to know the departments

a
Methodology

Warm-up: What departments and positions in a company do you know? The T lists all departments and positions the S name. With the jumbled list on the blackboard (the T may have to complete it) the T asks the S to say who is in charge of what, who is subordinate to whom, and which people and departments are of equal rank.

Key 🗝 **Key** 🗝 **Key** 🗝 **Key** 🗝

We have 9 departments.
Mr Stein is assistant to the managing director, Mr Thomas.
The marketing department comprises market research, advertising and sales.
Ms Carlo is secretary to Mr Thomas (Mr Thomas's secretary).
Mr Stiller is in charge of the marketing department.
Ms Yüksel reports to Mr Berger.
Mr Sievers is responsible for the financial side of the business.

b
Key 🗝 **Key** 🗝 **Key** 🗝 **Key** 🗝

1. stores department

2. personnel department
3. sales department
4. accounts department
5. advertising department
6. production department

c
Methodology

In this exercise, the S should explain what they believe their work will be in the individual departments. Possible duties:
- writing business letters (invoices, offers, orders, enquiries, etc.)
- doing the filing
- answering the phone
- doing calculations

Key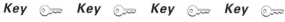

Examples:
I like/prefer working in the export department because it's the best place to learn about our business connections with foreign companies. It also offers the opportunity to speak to people from other countries and to travel a lot. In this way I can practise and improve my English.

I would really like to work in the purchasing department because there you learn all about suppliers and about how to get the best prices and the most favourable terms of payment and delivery. It's also interesting to visit potential suppliers and inspect their production facilities.

d
Methodology

Before doing this exercise the S should try to get an organigram of their companies. If this is not possible, the T could work out an organigram of a fictitious German company or use the organigram on page 12 (CB) for comparison.

Key

The key depends on the German organigrams (supplied by the S) which are to be compared with the English one.

e
Key

Student A: (possible questions)	Student B: (possible phrases)
1. What type of articles do you produce?	We produce ... (consumer electronics, computers, consumer goods, machines, spare parts for the car industry ...)
2. What is the location of your company?	It is situated in .../ between ... and ... /It's on the old site of ...
3. How many departments are there in your company?	There are ... departments.
4. How many employees does your firm have?	At present, we ... , but ...
5. Is English used much/ a little/at all in your company?	It's used .../not at all, because ...
6. Do you do business with foreign companies?	Yes, we do business with ..., because .../No, we don't ... because ...
7. Who is the person responsible for advertising in your firm? Who is in charge of PR?	That's Mr/Mrs/Miss ... He/She ...
8. Do you have flexitime in your company?	Yes, we do. I think it makes work a lot easier./ No, not yet.

C
Correspondence

a
Methodology

The S should study the Info-Box and the sample letter on page 14 and 15 before doing task **a**.

Key

1. letter head
2. date
3. complimentary close
4. enclosure
5. subject line

b
Key

1. Messrs
2. Dear Sirs*
3. We should like to
4. enclose
5. Yours faithfully
6. Enc.

* Please note that the salutation "Dear Sirs" is nowadays often substituted by "Dear Sir or Madam".

c
Methodology

Before doing this task, the S should study the Info-Box on page 17 (CB). The T may give some more examples of differences between a formal and an informal business letter or ask the S to think of examples themselves.

Key

Dear John

I'd like to thank you for your enquiry, but unfortunately we can't let you have the agency rights for your country.

Unit 1 · 9

We're already represented for all of Britain by Brunner & Bulmer, Kingsway, Midtown. You can get in touch with them and ask whether they would be interested to give you the sub-agency for Scotland.

I'm enclosing some of their leaflets for you.

I'm sorry that I can't give you a more positive reply.

All the best
Carl

d

Key

1. Registered mail is insured by the post office, and the recipient has to sign for it.
2. Newspapers, catalogues, etc. receive a preferential price from the post office, since they are sent in such great quantities. They have to be marked "Printed Matter".
3. A letter marked "urgent" is important and must be sent (and opened) as quickly as possible.
4. Letters, parcels, etc. with this marking remain at the post office until the recipient comes to collect them.
5. Mail sent by land and sea (not by air).
6. The same as 4.
7. Letters marked in this way are only to be opened/read by the addressee.
8. If the sender writes "Please forward" on the envelope, the post office must send the mail on to the addressee's new address, if known.

D
Phone calls:
Taking a message

a

Methodology

The listening comprehension exercise should be done in two steps: In step 1 (task **a**) the S are supposed to listen for the gist of the dialogue. In step 2 (task **b**) the S listen to the cassette again for particular information.
Before playing the cassette, the T could ask some introductory questions about phone calls.

Warm-up:
1. Have you ever made a phone call in English?
2. Have you ever received a phone call in English?
3. If so, were you able to get the information you needed (1.) and could you give the information requested (2.) without any problems?
4. Have you noticed any different accents on the phone? If so, which accent was the hardest to understand?

Key

A customer (Patrick Kelly of Bloom and Smith, Dublin) is trying to get in touch with Mr Acosta at H.A.T. to find out about the progress of his order for press plates. The trainee apologises; Mr Acosta is in Cologne for the day. However, he can take a message and promises to get the information to the customer by 7 o'clock that evening. The customer also asks for a quotation for a new order he is thinking of placing.

b

Key

1. Patrick Kelly of Bloom and Smith, Dublin is calling H.A.T.
2. Kelly wants to know what is happening with his order.
3. The order No. is A 354 of September 6th.
4. It is getting late (there are only 21 days for delivery left) and Kelly wants reassurance that his order will be executed in time.
5. He can't get the reply immediately, because Mr Acosta is in Cologne.

Additional questions:

1. How many people are speaking, and what are their names? (Kelly and an employee of H.A.T.)
2. Where are they? (Kelly is in Ireland, the employee in Remscheid.)
3. How would you classify the first part of the conversation (enquiry, order, complaint, etc.)? (It's an enquiry about the order status.)
4. What type is the second part of the conversation? (An enquiry that might lead to a new order.)
5. Is Mr Acosta taking a day off? (No, he's in H.A.T.'s Cologne branch.)
6. Till when can the customer be reached, and where? (Till 7 o'clock, and probably in his office, since the number is on the order form.)
7. How will H.A.T. get the details of the new order? (By fax.)

c

Key

Model dialogue:

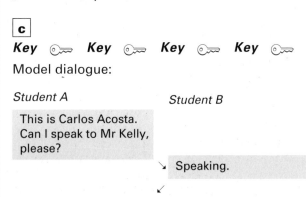

Student A: This is Carlos Acosta. Can I speak to Mr Kelly, please?

Student B: Speaking.

Sorry I couldn't call you back earlier, but I was in Cologne.

That's all right, I know that you have a lot of work, too. I wanted to find out what's happening to my order. That's No. A 354.

Order No. A 354 is just being checked. We've planned the shipment for 16 October. It'll be sent by air freight.

That's fine, it should arrive here by the 20th.

I heard you want a new quotation. Could you give me the details?

Yes, I need a quotation for some new press plates, but I'd like it before the beginning of November.

I think we can manage it before that time. We'll deal with it when we receive the details.

That would be fine. Thank you for calling. Goodbye.

Goodbye.

d

Key *Key* *Key* *Key*

Model dialogue:

B: John Thomas & Co., Gillieland, Victoria. Can I help you?
A: Good morning. My name is ..., and I'm calling from Germany. We saw your advert for eucalyptus oils in the *South Australian Exporter* and we would like to get some more information.
B: Hold the line, please. I'll put you through to Mr Dundee, our export manager. Hello ...
A: Yes? Is that the export manager?
B: No. I'm sorry, but he's just gone out. Would you like to leave a message?
A: Yes, please. Would you ask Mr Dundee to send us a catalogue and a price list of eucal-yptus oils?
B: I'll tell him to see to your request as soon as he gets back.
A: Thank you very much. Goodbye.
B: You're welcome. Goodbye.

e

Key *Key* *Key* *Key*

1. The individual phone number inside a company belonging to one office, person or department.
2. The telephone number for a specific area, town, etc. It must be dialled when phoning from outside this area.
3. The telephone number for a specific country. It must be dialled when phoning from outside this country.
4. The book containing all the names, phone numbers and addresses of the subscribers in a specific area.
5. The person receiving this type of call will have to pay for it.
6. Here, the caller instructs the telephone company to contact a specific person and call him/her back when this person is on the line.
7. A glass-sided cubicle containing a public telephone.
8. The telephone exchange in a company.
9. The person at the telephone exchange who makes the connection for you.
10. A phone call outside your own area.

E

The company secretary

Methodology

One major purpose of this part is to get the S to start using dictionaries regularly. The S should keep in mind that different dictionaries may give different meanings and spellings (British English/American English, e.g.: "traveller/ traveler, theatre/theater, tyre/tire"."Organize/ organise" are used indiscriminately, although the "ize" ending is taken to be more English) and different splittings of words or syllabification (e.g. in-hu-man/in-hum-an).

> **i The Company Secretary**
>
> This position does not exist in Germany, although most dictionaries translate it as „Schriftführer" or „Syndikus". The CS is generally the third-most important person in a company, after the director and the treasurer. He/She is responsible for all official publications of the company and for the company's charter.

a

Key 🗝 *Key* 🗝 *Key* 🗝 *Key* 🗝

Nach dem britischen Gesetz muss jede Firma eine/n Sekretär/in ernennen. Zu dessen/deren Aufgabengebiet gehört u. a. die Leitung der Rechtsabteilung. Es gibt keine genaue Stellenbeschreibung, jedoch schreibt man der Stelle die Aufgaben eines Vorstandsmitglieds zu. Die typischen Aufgaben werden in die sogenannten Kernaufgaben und die zusätzlichen Aufgaben aufgeteilt.

Zu den Kernaufgaben gehören:

- Die Unterstützung des Direktoriums in rechtlichen und verwaltungstechnischen Fragen. D. h. dafür zu sorgen, dass regelmäßige Vorstandssitzungen abgehalten und die dort gefassten Ergebnisse umfassend aufgezeichnet werden.
- Ferner darauf zu achten, dass Entscheidungen und Anweisungen des Vorstands ausgeführt werden (z. B. als Verbindungsmann zur Börse, zum Management, zu den Aktionären und Institutionen).
- Die Einhaltung von Statuten und Regularien.
- Wo es angebracht ist, sich für die Interessen der Aktionäre einzusetzen.

Zu den zusätzlichen Aufgaben gehört die verantwortliche Kontrolle über die Abteilungen, auch wenn zahlreiche Unternehmensabteilungen ihre eigenen Manager haben.

b

Key 🗝 *Key* 🗝 *Key* 🗝 *Key* 🗝

The company secretary is an officer of the company, that is, he/she is responsible for the administration in the firm. An office secretary, on the other hand, only works in the office, dealing with correspondence, making appointments, etc.

c

Key 🗝 *Key* 🗝 *Key* 🗝 *Key* 🗝

1. stock exchange (Börse):
   The institution at which shares are traded in (bought and sold).
2. board of directors (Verwaltungsrat/Firmenvorstand):
   These decide on major policy decisions and those affecting the future of a company.
3. shareholder (Aktionär/in):
   A shareholder owns a share (Aktie) or shares in a company, and is entitled to vote at general meetings (Generalversammlungen).
4. legal department (juristische Abteilung, Rechtsabteilung):
   The department in a company that deals with all the questions concerning the law.
5. core duties („Kernaufgaben"):
   These are the main duties that must be carried out by a person.

Unit 2
Production

Contents/Targets:

This unit deals with types of production, reasons for production, modern production methods, and, in the communications section, telexes and faxes. It describes a German manufacturer of technical products, Herrmann KG, and the role modern computerised manufacturing and quality-assurance processes play in this firm and others.

Starter: The S are shown some modern products and they are asked questions about their possible origin. The S learn to describe products in terms of origin, production costs, and quality.

A: The S learn how to describe production strategies and how to compare products and product features.

B: The S learn some essential terms regarding modern quality control and automation, relating these to their own companies. A letter of apology is also included for translation.

C: This part contains some typical fax messages, as well as instructions for writing telexes and faxes.

D: In this section, the S hear a complaint on the phone (Listening comprehension). In the following role play they have to work out a larger proportion of the sentences themselves than in the first role play in Unit 1.

E: Here, the (more advanced) S read an authentic English newspaper text on a technical subject.

Starter

Methodology

The T could use some introductory questions (e.g. What make is your cassette player/pocket calculator/video recorder? Where is/was this product produced? What made you buy it?) to elicit the idea that many foreign products are lower-priced here than German ones. Alternatively, the T could write "Made in Japan/Korea/China ..." on the blackboard and ask the S to list corresponding products under these countries.

Key ⚿ *Key* ⚿ *Key* ⚿ *Key* ⚿

1. Various answers are possible here: e.g. clothes: France or Italy; video camera: Japan, Korea, Taiwan; perfume: France, Italy or India; wine: France, Spain, Italy, Germany, Australia, America (California); handbags: Spain, Italy; shoes: Spain, Italy, India or Thailand; TV set: Japan, Korea, Taiwan, Germany, The Netherlands

2. As superior product quality is no longer a privilege of the highly industrialized countries – in fact more and more European or American companies have their products made in Asia, Africa or South America – a generalizing statement about the reputation of a country in terms of product quality should be avoided. It should be mentioned, though, that many countries which used to have a "bad reputation" regarding their product quality have caught up with their competitors in the last few years.
   The countries of the Third World and countries like Portugal or Spain (depending on the product) are known for their low production costs.

3. Low costs of land, labour, industrial sites etc.

4. As consumers often think of the price first, the domestic competition may be forced out of business, unless they are helped either by subsidies from their own government or by stricter import regulations.

A
Production strategies – Quality or design?

Methodology

With the books closed, the T writes the words "quality" and "design" on the blackboard. The S are then asked to name ideas which they associate with these words, e.g. (quality): high price and durability.

Key ⚿ *Key* ⚿ *Key* ⚿ *Key* ⚿

1. Formerly, companies were more price-oriented, while today, they concentrate on market research, i.e. the customers' wishes.

2. Product-oriented in the sense of the text means that companies produce the products which the market requires by using market research methods.

3. See text (last 13 lines in column 1).

Unit 2 · 13

4. Possible products: shoes, watches, frames for glasses, jewellery
5. "Made in Germany" (used to be a general badge of reliability and it still is for many products), "Made in Solingen" (knives, cutlery), "Made in Switzerland" (watches), "Bottled in France (wine)", "Product of Jamaica" (rum)

b
Methodology

The S should discuss the importance of price, reliability and appearance and design with regard to the four products. As they will have different priorities, the S should be prepared to explain these.

c
Methodology

In this exercise the S are asked to discuss the importance of different product features.

d
Methodology

Here, the S are asked to think of the products of the companies where they are working (or where they have worked). Perhaps they can bring some product descriptions or advertising material where the most prominent product features are highlighted.

B
Quality control and production technologies

1. Quality control and automation

a
Key 🗝 *Key* 🗝 *Key* 🗝 *Key* 🗝

1 announce, 2 improved, 3 lowered, 4 controllers, 5 keyboard, 6 commands, 7 "off", 8 measures, 9 innovation, 10 downtime, 11 inefficient

b
Key 🗝 *Key* 🗝 *Key* 🗝 *Key* 🗝

1 virtually, 2 speed-up, 3 quantity, 4 great, 5 modern, 6 contaminated, 7 dismiss

c
Key 🗝 *Key* 🗝 *Key* 🗝 *Key* 🗝

1. Herrmann KG have improved their safety record and lowered their pollution level. They have also increased their production by 18%.
2. It keeps people away from the dangerous production lines.
3. Automation and remote control keep people away from the machines which can cause accidents.
4. Quality assurance measures and modern machines have made it possible to reduce the waste.
5. Older machines are less precise, run hotter, increase the heat pollution and require more dangerous working fluids, thus creating more waste.

d
Key 🗝 *Key* 🗝 *Key* 🗝 *Key* 🗝

Advantages: greater precision, fewer costs for labour, insurance, and premises (no extra space required for workers' rooms, etc.), the machines can run practically 24 hours per day and don't ask for overtime or holiday pay.

Disadvantages: High costs for the new machines, redundant workers.

e
Key 🗝 *Key* 🗝 *Key* 🗝 *Key* 🗝

The answer depends on the S.

2. Modern production technology

a
Methodology

Before doing task **a** the T could ask the S an introductory question: What do the abbreviations CAD and CAM stand for? (Key: **C**omputer-**A**ided **D**esign/**C**omputer-**A**ided **M**anufacture)

Key 🗝 *Key* 🗝 *Key* 🗝 *Key* 🗝

This is a diagram showing the interactions between the elements in computerised manufacturing. All operations from designing a product to delivering it are controlled by the CPU (Central Processor Unit).

b
Methodology

Depending on the class, this exercise can either be done as a reading comprehension or a listening comprehension. In the latter case, two S read the dialogue while the others make notes to answer the questions in exercise **c**.

c
Key 🗝 *Key* 🗝 *Key* 🗝 *Key* 🗝

1. The small switches are used in machine tools and transfer lines. When the machine has reached the limit of its travel, it is stopped by

the switch. If this doesn't happen, either the workpiece or the machine will probably be damaged.
2. When CAD is used, there is no need for expensive prototype machines or models. All movements can be seen and/or calculated using the computer. This is the practical application of virtual reality.
3. The advantages are that there is no chance for human error to take place, as the computer does all the "thinking". It also saves personnel costs and makes sure that every part made is exactly the same as the original. Possible disadvantages might be: False programming, leading to a whole production run being scrap, machine breakdowns not being noticed until it is too late, the risk of strikes because staff is laid off.

d
Key
1. CAM – E *computer - aided manufacturing*
2. CAD – C *computer aided design*
3. VDU – B *visual display unit*
4. CIM – A *computer integrated manufacturing*
5. CNC – D *computer numeric control*

e
Methodology
The S should think of their companies' determining factors in the employment of new technologies, such as the degree of precision or the speed of manufacture required.

3. A delay in production

Methodology
The S should be warned that bosses are considerably more intolerant than teachers in the matter of exact translations. In the harsh commercial reality, all that really counts is 100 % correctness of the contents. So confusing delivery dates or terms of payment is a quick way to get into trouble.

Key ⚬— *Key* ⚬— *Key* ⚬— *Key* ⚬—

Sehr geehrter Herr Herrmann,

wir versuchen schon seit vorigen Mittwoch uns mit Ihnen in Verbindung zu setzen. Es wurde uns aber von Ihrem Büropersonal mitgeteilt, dass Sie geschäftlich unterwegs waren.

Wir bedauern Ihnen mitteilen zu müssen, dass es bei der Ausführung Ihres Auftrages Nr. 232/b vom 20. April zu einer Verzögerung kommen wird, und zwar wegen eines Schadens bei einer Sonderfräsmaschine in unserer Fabrik.

Diese Maschine war für die Herstellung der Platinen unserer Grenzschalter unerlässlich und wir waren bis Ende letzter Woche nicht in der Lage, einen Ersatz zu finden.

Die Ersatzmaschine ist nun eingetroffen und wir werden die Produktion innerhalb von zwei Tagen wieder aufnehmen. Es wird leider eine einwöchige Verspätung bei der endgültigen Auslieferung der Platinen geben, obwohl wir Ihrer Bestellung den äußersten Vorrang gewähren.

Wir hoffen, dass Sie unsere Entschuldigung für etwaige Unannehmlichkeiten, die Ihnen dies bereitet annehmen. Wir versichern Ihnen, dass wir alles unternehmen werden um zu gewährleisten, dass Ihre Aufträge nie wieder verspätet ausgeführt werden.

Mit freundlichen Grüßen

C
Fax and telex messages

Methodology
Part C is intended to make the S familiar with different layouts of faxes. The S should realize that every company has its own layout for their fax sheets and that all fax sheets have certain elements in common. The S could also bring fax sheets from the companies where they are working for comparison and discussion.

a
Key ⚬— *Key* ⚬— *Key* ⚬— *Key* ⚬—
Sender, addressee, date, fax No., number of pages, salutation, text, complimentary close

b
Key ⚬— *Key* ⚬— *Key* ⚬— *Key* ⚬—
Depends on the S.

c
Methodology
The S should invent any missing details when writing the fax.

Key 🗝 Key 🗝 Key 🗝 Key 🗝
(Model Fax)

FAX

Büromöbel Kerner GmbH
Hansaring 222
51287 Köln
Tel.: 0221/565493
Fax: 0221/565378

To: Toby's Office Supplies
From: Ms Klein/Büromöbel Kerner GmbH
Fax: 0044/113/247986
Date: 5 April, ...
Number of pages including this page: 1

Dear Sir or Madam (Dear Sirs),

Please send us your recent catalogue and price list to the above address.

Thank you in advance.

Yours faithfully,

((Signature))

---

d

Key 🗝 Key 🗝 Key 🗝 Key 🗝
ATTN = attention, RE/REF = reference, PLS = please, ASAP = as soon as possible, APPROX = approximately, DOCS = documents, NXT = next, ETA = estimated time of arrival, RPLY = reply, YR = your

e

Key 🗝 Key 🗝 Key 🗝 Key 🗝
Telex to Herrmann KG

Please send (a) quotation (with) best prices for 2,000 industrial vacuum cleaners for hospital system in Nepal. (Goods must be) delivered FOB Hamburg including tropical packing and spares for 2 years.

Royal Hospitals Board, Nepal

f

Key 🗝 Key 🗝 Key 🗝 Key 🗝
1. Dear Fred,

   Thank you for your advice of dispatch of 20 April.

   We expect the goods next week at NY Port (Port of New York).

   After inspection, we will remit the invoice amount.

   Please send the certificate of origin for our customer to get the import licence.

   Regards,

   Bill

2. With reference to your order No. 225/95 dated 25th July, this can only be delivered in 2 months. There has been a breakdown in

16 · Unit 2

production due to material shortage, which led to the delay.

We will inform you of the exact delivery time and grant you 5% discount for this delay.

Please telex us for more details.

Order 226/94 will be on time.

The shipment will be FOB by Brown & Co., Birmingham, in containers, payment cash, and insurance paid for by you.

Methodology

The S could be requested to write the reply out in clear text first, and then condense it to a telex text.

Key ○— *Key* ○— *Key* ○— *Key* ○—
(Possible replies)

1. THNX FR LETTR DD 19/5 STOP UNDSTND DLAY AND ACCPT IT IF U GRNT 5 O/O DISCNT STOP THS MUST NOT HPN AGN STOP RGDS

2. THNX FR LETTR DD 19/5 STOP CANT ACCPT DLAY AS MUST DLVR IMMED AFTR RCPT SWTCHS STOP CVERNG RQURMNTS OTHR SUPPLR IF U CANT DLVR STOP RGDS

D

Phone calls:
A complaint about a delay

Methodology

Here, the S should listen for the gist of the phone call and try to find out the reason for the delay.

Key ○— *Key* ○— *Key* ○— *Key* ○—
The delay took place because there had been a mistake in the design department. This was only discovered two days ago.

Key ○— *Key* ○— *Key* ○— *Key* ○—
1. It is order No. 653/2 of 23rd May.
2. The reference number is B75.
3. He only found this out two days ago (or before the phone call).
4. Insurance companies are not very happy when they have to pay out on an insurance claim.
5. He suggests that Gold and Piper buy from an alternative supplier.

Role play

Methodology

Before starting the role play the S should be given some time for preparation. They should use the prompts given and invent any missing details. Make sure the S use the right tenses!

Key ○— *Key* ○— *Key* ○— *Key* ○—
Model dialogue:

Student A   *Student B*

Good morning, Mr/Ms ... (student's name or any other name) This is ... of Herrmann KG in Rosenheim, Germany.

              Good morning, Mr/Ms ...

You visited us two days ago, and placed an order for 500 caravan and camping refrigerators.

              Yes, are there any problems with the order?

Well, there's been a fire in our warehouse, and all our stocks have been destroyed.

              Oh, I'm sorry to hear that. Will delivery still be possible?

I'm afraid it will be impossible to supply you with the refrigerators on time.

              But we need the refrigerators urgently. What can we do?

We're sorry, but all we can do is to recommend another supplier. That's Paas & Co. in Sindelfingen.

> Could you fax us their address and phone number, please?

> Certainly. I'll have it faxed to you within one hour. I would like to apologize again for the inconvenience, but we'll be back in production and able to supply again in about 4 weeks' time.

> Thank you for your help. We'll get in touch with you as soon as we need further refrigerators. Goodbye.

> Goodbye.

E
Designed, built and tested on computer

a

Methodology

If possible, the S should read the text and try to give a German summary without looking up any unknown words.

Key ⚬— *Key* ⚬— *Key* ⚬— *Key* ⚬—

Rolls-Royce, der Hersteller von Düsentriebwerken, wird als erste Firma ein neues Düsentriebwerk am Computerbildschirm entwickeln, bauen und testen. Die Firma ist gerade dabei, mit der Unterstützung von Computervision, einem Spezialisten auf dem Gebiet des CAD (Computer-aided design), ein „Elektronisches Produktdefinitionssystem" (Electronic Product Definition = EPD) einzuführen. Rolls-Royce verspricht sich von diesem neuen System Einsparungen in Millionenhöhe, obwohl zunächst einmal Software für dreidimensionale Darstellungen für mehr als 14 Millionen (Pfund) eingekauft wurde. Die Einsparungen sollen in erster Linie dadurch erzielt werden, dass keine Modelle mehr benötigt werden um die neuen Triebwerke zu testen. Notwendige Änderungen bei der Entwicklung der Triebwerke können mit der Computervision-Software in wenigen Tagen durchgeführt werden. Mit Modellen würde dies Wochen dauern. Trent, das neueste Triebwerk von Rolls-Royce, ist das Flaggschiff der Firma und das leistungsfähigste Triebwerk der Welt. Der Airbus A330 hat bereits die Testflüge mit dem neuen Triebwerk begonnen und die Boeing 777 wird 1996 ihren Dienst mit dem Trent-Triebwerk aufnehmen. Etwa ein Viertel der beiden neuen Flugzeugtypen soll mit dem Trent-Triebwerk ausgestattet werden.

Jim Dann, ein Experte im Bau von Flugzeugmotoren, ist sich sicher, dass sich die Investition in Computer auszahlen wird.

Bei der Entwicklung des Trent-Triebwerks wird CADDS 5-Software benutzt, um die Montage aller Teile in einem Prozess zu simulieren, der „digitale Vormontage" (Digital Pre-Assembly) genannt wird. Selbst bei einem weniger komplizierten Triebwerk wie dem RB 211 muss auf diese Weise bereits die Montage von mehr als 18 000 Teilen simuliert werden.

Die Investitionen in die Computerfirma können nach Aussage von Rolls innerhalb der nächsten sieben Jahre durchaus die Größenordnung von 40 Millionen (Pfund) erreichen.

Dass sich EPD und die „digitale Vormontage" nicht nur auf Flugzeugtriebwerke beschränken, beweisen solche Produkte wie der Land Rover Discovery, der CD-Player, der Airbus und die Sprintschuhe von Carl Lewis.

b

Key ⚬— *Key* ⚬— *Key* ⚬— *Key* ⚬—

1. EPD is electronic product definition. This means that the parts of a product are designed on a computer screen and then, using the computer, checked to see if they will fit together properly. This avoids problems which can arise e.g. when drawings are misread or two teams work from different bases.
2. The parts can be checked for function without having to produce expensive prototypes and models.
3. The model-maker here produces his models using software, not metal or wood.
4. This is the general trend since it saves money.
5. (Lines 60–68) The system is being used for a great number of applications.

c

Key ⚬— *Key* ⚬— *Key* ⚬— *Key* ⚬—

1. Get an advantage over
2. A full-sized model of a part produced later, generally in the aviation industry. The mock-up is generally used for getting an impression of the appearance, checking the fit of parts, and generally seeing whether anything is obviously wrong.
3. A workstation (here) is a computer terminal.
4. Mounted on (attached to)
5. To be worthwhile in the long term (when used for a sufficient length of time)
6. A good helper, one that makes work go faster

UNIT 3
Purchasing and storekeeping

Contents/Targets

Unit 3 centres on Paul Meyer, a young employee of the German company Schmidt & Co. in Heiligenhaus, who has been sent to their English subsidiary Hunt & Forrester (H & F). The unit not only shows the organization and work of a typical store in an industrial business but also how procurement can be effected including a contract of sale and commercial letters.

Starter: The S are shown several parts of a car in order to start a discussion on who produced them – a supplier or the car manufacturer.

A: Here, the S get to know purchasing procedures, the essential parts of a contract of sale and how potential suppliers are chosen.

B: The S learn about a possible structure of an industrial store, the working methods in the stores and the terms and forms used in a store.

C: Section C introduces the different types of business letters related to purchasing.

D: The S learn how to make an appointment on the phone by doing a listening comprehension exercise and a role play.

E: Starting with a more advanced text, the S learn about stock levels and how to interpret a stock control graph.

Starter

a

Methodology
Warm-up:

As not all S will be familiar with the car industry, they could, before starting exercise **a**, form groups according to the branches where they are working. The S in each group should then make a list of all parts their companies purchase from suppliers.

Key Key Key Key
Depending on the car manufacturer, all parts in the pictures could be bought. Parts like brake pads, door handles, steering wheels, tyres, exhaust pipes and shock absorbers are very likely to be purchased from suppliers.

b

Key Key Key Key

1. A lot of components are produced in the Far East (electronic parts, tyres), for instance in China, Taiwan, Korea, Malaysia; other components come from the Czech Republic (brake pads); UK (gearboxes and exhaust pipes); China, Germany, USA, Spain (door handles and car locks).
2. Some parts can be stored on shelves (dashboards, exhaust pipes), others are simply stored in box pallets (Gitterboxpaletten) (for example brake pads), tyres are just laid down on the floor in a certain section of the store.
3.

advantages	disadvantages
lower costs	quality problems
higher flexibility	insecure political situation
*	possible delays in delivery

4. The more components are bought from abroad, the cheaper the production of the final product becomes at home.

A
Choice of suppliers – Essential parts of a contract of sale

a

Key Key Key Key

1. beneficial
2. crucial
3. quality assurance
4. a potential/ prospective supplier
5. ecologically neutral or beneficial
6. reliability
7. willingness
8. price aspect

b

Key Key Key Key

1. false
2. false
3. false
4. true
5. true

c

Key Key Key Key

1. The exact product description (quality), the quantity, the price and possible discounts, the terms of delivery and payment, insurance and packing.
2. The supplier's reliability, a guarantee on the products, and environmentally-friendly production methods may easily outweigh the price aspect.
3. With an ever increasing environmental awareness among consumers, an environmentally-friendly production may be a decisive selling point.
* (in-company manufacture may lead to capacity problems)

Unit 3 · 19

d

Key 🗝 *Key* 🗝 *Key* 🗝 *Key* 🗝

The terms of the contract of sale, constant high quality of the products, reliable delivery, ecological aspects of the products and their production.

e

Methodology

Here, the S should try to compare the criteria already mentioned with the criteria their training companies take into account when looking for new suppliers.

B
Storekeeping

i

The S should be able to comprehend how the general process of storekeeping can be carried out. (The case mentioned in this book has got nearly all the general features of storekeeping.)
The goods arrive at the Receiving Department (Warenannahme), where they are identified and inspected by means of the delivery note (Lieferschein) and the waybill (Frachtbrief).
Then computer printouts are attached to the goods that show in which part of the store the goods are to be put. Before they reach their final destination on the shelves they are put into the stores awaiting location area (Wareneingangsbereich).
An essential storing principle is the first in-first out method. It says that new parts are stored at the back and the old ones in front in order to avoid parts being forgotten, becoming ruined or out of date. Before the articles are transported into the warehouse, a small accompanying card (bin ticket) is attached showing the part number and a description as well as the arrival date of the parts.
After that, the articles are transported to their usual place and packed onto the shelves. The stores personnel record all incoming and outgoing goods on a store/stock card (Lagerfachkarte).

a

Key

1. is a place where the goods delivered arrive (Warenannahme)
2. is a list of goods being delivered, given to the customer with the goods (Lieferschein)
3. is a list of goods carried, made out by the carrier (Frachtbrief)
4. is a written notice to a customer giving details of goods ordered and shipped but not yet delivered (Versandanzeige)
5. is a note needed for the purchasing department, which compares the details with the ones on the purchase order; another copy goes to the accounts department (Warenempfangsbescheinigung)
6. are components that have to be bought/purchased
7. is a special place in the storeroom where the inspected goods wait before they are placed onto their correct shelf
8. is used to mark bins, boxes, etc.
9. is an article
10. is a card that records incoming and outgoing goods and the up-to-date stock level (also stock card) (Lagerfachkarte)
11. It shows the current quantity that is on stock. (aktueller Lagerbestand)
12. is a label that shows what is in the container (Erkennungsmarke)

b

Key 🗝 *Key* 🗝 *Key* 🗝 *Key* 🗝

1. advice note
2. delivery note
3. waybill
4. goods received note
5. bin ticket
6. identification tag

c

Key 🗝 *Key* 🗝 *Key* 🗝 *Key* 🗝

1. The goods are checked for type, quantity, quality and packing against the delivery note and the waybill.
2. They have to fill out the goods received notes correctly and distribute them.
3. Because of their own products' high quality standard.
4. It is attached to the parts and accompanies them until they are put into the stores. The ticket states the part number, the description of the goods and the arrival date.
5. It is determined by requisition from production or sales department. The staff then has to fill in the stock card.
6. A principle of storing goods which makes sure that the goods which are first stored are the first goods that leave the stores again.

d

Key 🗝 *Key* 🗝 *Key* 🗝 *Key* 🗝

The answer depends on the S' own experience.

1. A goods received note

Methodology

The T asks some S to read the information in the book.
After that, the S are asked to do the matching exercise by translating the German shipment details into English.

Key *Key* *Key* *Key*
1. A, 2. C, 3. D, 4. B, 5. E, 6. F, 7. G, 8. H

2. A stock card

Methodology

Here, the S are asked to fill in a copied stock card using the information given in the book. As a further exercise, the T can now transfer the task to the S' own company (e.g. Which articles and details are normally entered on a stock card in your firm?).

> *i*
>
> In the last few years more and more companies have introduced computers in their stores' administration (management).

C
Enquiries, offers, orders, acknowledgements of order

Methodology

The S should study Paul's enquiry before doing exercise **a**. Unknown words can be written on the blackboard.

a

Methodology

The S are asked to study the phrases in the box on page 43 before replacing the parts in bold type of the enquiry on page 42.

Key *Key* *Key* *Key*
We see from your advertisement in ...
(we are interested in ...) – we require ...
(Could you send us ...) – We would be grateful if you could send us ...
(We would further like to know about ...) – Please let us know ... / We would appreciate information on ...
(We look forward to receiving ...) – We look forward to an early reply.

b

Key *Key* *Key* *Key*
Dear Sir or Madam (Dear Sirs),

We have seen your advertisement in the latest issue of *Modern Office Furniture*.

As we have received enquiries from our customers for computer furniture, we should be pleased if you could send us your latest catalogue and price list.

We would also be grateful if you could state your delivery terms.

We look forward to hearing from you soon.

Yours faithfully,

c

Methodology

The S are asked to use the phrases from the box. Any missing details should be invented.

Key *Key* *Key* *Key*
The letter depends on the S.

d

Methodology

The S should study the two quotations thoroughly and list the main differences.
If help is required, the T could refer to the enquiry on page 42 again.

Key *Key* *Key* *Key*
Quotation 2 is more favourable because the price is lower, the delivery time is shorter, and the terms of payment are better.

e

Key *Key* *Key* *Key*

	No. 1 *American*	No. 2 *English*
	catalog	catalogue
	Dear Mr Meyer**:**	Dear Mr Meyer**,**
	May 6, 19..	10 May 19..
	Yours very truly	Yours sincerely

f

Key *Key* *Key* *Key*

	American	*English*
e.g.	first floor	ground floor
	elevator	lift
	color	colour
	favor	favour
	eraser	rubber
	inquiry	enquiry
	vacation	holiday
	collect call	transfer charge call
	fall	autumn

g

Key *Key* *Key* *Key*

1. Quotation

Dear Mr Sambu,

We thank you for your enquiry of 14 April, 19.. concerning exhaust pipes.
There would be no trouble in supplying the required pipes.
We are pleased to quote as follows:

    exhaust pipes XU/1521/14 --,-- DM each.

We offer a special quantity discount of 10% for orders exceeding 200 pipes.
Furthermore, we can grant you a 1-year guarantee on the products.
Delivery can be effected within 2 weeks after receipt of order.
Our terms of payment are: cash within 14 days of invoice date.

Please find enclosed our latest catalogue.

Yours sincerely,
(signature)

Wagner Autozubehör GmbH

Enc.

2. Order

Dear ...,

Thank you for your quotation of ... concerning exhaust pipes.
We are pleased to place the following order:

    250 exhaust pipes XU/1521/14

We agree to the conditions in your quotation.
Please acknowledge this order as soon as possible.

Yours sincerely,
George Sambu

Harare Car Center

3. Acknowledgement of order

Dear Mr Sambu,

We acknowlege with thanks your order of ... for 250 exhaust pipes XU/1521/14.
The consignment will be dispatched to you by sea freight next week.
We hope that you will be completely satisfied with our goods and look forward to receiving further orders in the future.

Yours sincerely,
(signature)

Wagner Autozubehör GmbH

D Phone calls: Making an appointment

Methodology

The following listening comprehension should be made in two steps:
In task **a** the S are asked to listen for gist and in task **b** the S listen for the details.
In a role play the S (2 or 3 pairs) can simulate the telephone conversation between Paul and Mr Wirestone's secretary sitting back to back. The S should make some notes before practising.

a

Key *Key* *Key* *Key*

1. A customer of Paul's firm is a leading car producer with a high quality standard.
2. Mr Wirestone approves the visit, because he prefers doing business with someone he knows personally.
3. Mr Wirestone invites them to lunch because he wants to create a friendly and personal atmosphere to conclude the contract.

b

Key *Key* *Key* *Key*

That's a very good idea.
And we'd be glad to welcome you.
I personally think it's always better to do business with someone you know.
Yes, that suits me.
We'll be pleased to show you our plant and discuss all your questions.

c

Key *Key* *Key* *Key*

Model dialogue:

Student A (Paul) *Student B (Secretary)*

> Good afternoon, this is Paul Meyer of H&F, Birmingham, speaking. Could I speak to Mr Wirestone's secretary?

> Speaking. Hello, Mr Meyer. What can I do for you?

> I've just returned from lunch and found the message on my desk that Mr Wirestone is ill.

Ah, I see. I'm afraid Mr Wirestone won't be able to keep the date. We'll have to fix a new one.

Well, let me have a look at my diary. Is Wednesday morning, the 25th OK?

Oh, I'm sorry. Mr Wirestone is having a department meeting first and then he's going to lunch with a business friend.

What about Thursday the 26th, at noon?

Well, Mr Wirestone has got a meeting with the sales manager till 1 pm, but then he'll be able to welcome you. Does 2 pm suit you?

Oh, yes indeed. 2 pm is fine.

So that's settled then. I'm just making a note of it for Mr Wirestone.

Thank you very much. Bye for now.

Good bye, Mr Meyer. And thank you for calling.

E
Surplus stock

a

Key 🗝 *Key* 🗝 *Key* 🗝 *Key* 🗝
higher costs/reduced production/job cuts/plants have to be closed down

b

Key 🗝 *Key* 🗝 *Key* 🗝 *Key* 🗝
The agricultural commodities market in Europe (e.g. butter mountain, wine lake, milk surplus, fruit surplus)

c

Methodology

Before answering the questions on the graph, the T could ask the S to describe the graph (e.g. the line rises/falls/reaches a high/low).

For a more precise description of graphs see page 58 (CB).

Key 🗝 *Key* 🗝 *Key* 🗝 *Key* 🗝
1. 3 (min. stock level), 9 (max. stock level)
2. 5
3. 7
4. One week

d

Key
1. vertical
2. slanting
3. re-order level
4. lead time
5. minimum stock level

Unit 3 · 23

Unit 4
Marketing

Contents/Targets

This unit covers various aspects of the marketing mix. After attempting to present an outline of the marketing spectrum, the unit takes up the example of Wunder showers, a German company that tries to introduce its products on the British market and therefore has to take decisions about the marketing of its products in the new market.

Starter: The S are confronted with a cartoon that gives a mock definition of the marketing process.

A: Looking at two product launches, the S learn about the components of the marketing mix and how to express their views on possible variations of this mix. Additionally they are introduced to the reasons for the Wunder launch in GB.

B: The S get acquainted with the Wunder shower range and find out about describing products.

C: The S get an understanding of the marketing mix for the Wunder shower launch and write a guided meeting report (the minutes of a meeting). With the help of the marketing research underlying the Wunder market introduction, the S get an introduction to describing graphs and figures and the equipment needed for a presentation.

D: The S are confronted with a typical market research interview for the launch of Wunder showers, which gives them help for structuring and conducting a mock market research interview. They are also taught to use polite phrases when doing so.

E: An introduction to copy analysis is provided and has to be applied to three shower ads. Moreover, some general advertising vocabulary is introduced and the S are asked about the communication media used in their own company.

Starter

Marketing is ...

Methodology

Depending on their background knowledge of marketing from their business classes, the S might want more or less help from the T, especially when it comes to answering **b** and **c**.

a

Key ⌬ *Key* ⌬ *Key* ⌬ *Key* ⌬

Two stone age businessmen (similar to the Flintstones) – naked apart from skirts, cuffs, glasses and ties – meet in front of two palm trees in the jungle. The bigger and fatter one (the seller), carries a big package on his head which the leaner character (the buyer) points at. The seller then simply drops the package on the buyer, who gets squashed in the process.

b

Key ⌬ *Key* ⌬ *Key* ⌬ *Key* ⌬

The cartoonist wants to poke fun at the definition of marketing given in the cartoon's text. This condensed definition oversimplifies the marketing process: It is not just the literal "simple enough" dumping of goods on the buyer and the market as the cartoon would make us believe, but a rather complex affair. The cartoon makes the reader think about the validity of definitions and the meaning of marketing in particular.

c

Key ⌬ *Key* ⌬ *Key* ⌬ *Key* ⌬

As this is a matter of personal opinion no generalised answer is possible here. However, depending on the S' background knowledge, answers might refer to the execution of the cartoon itself and/or its intention.

A
Two case studies

Case study 1:
The new CWK video recorder

Methodology

Before letting the S read the text on the CWK video recorder, make sure they have understood the introductory text on page 50.
Point out that words most likely to cause difficulties in the text are explained in **a**; reading the text and doing the exercise should therefore be done together.
In order to get a better understanding of the complex meaning of the term "Marketing", the T could draw up a mind map on the blackboard asking the S to name words/terms that come to their minds when hearing the following key words (in bold type).

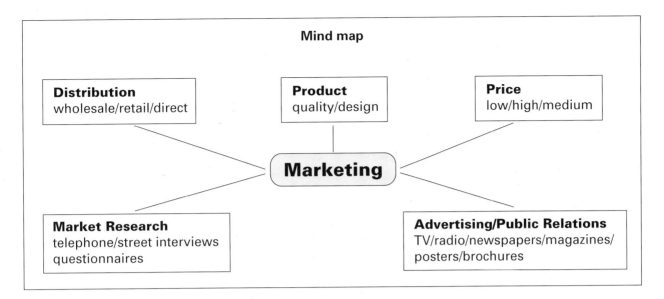

a

Key 🗝 *Key* 🗝 *Key* 🗝 *Key* 🗝

1. to launch   2. to be backed   3. corporate   4. full-feature   5. retail outlet

b

Key 🗝 *Key* 🗝 *Key* 🗝 *Key* 🗝

product	price	place (distribution)	promotion
CWK C 120 video recorder	high price (£1,500)	retail outlets	corporate promotion campaign including:
professional line product			£6m advertising campaign in special interest magazines
full-feature			stands at trade fairs
two independent drives and separate recording and playback heads for high speed copying			sales representatives visiting retailers and professional users
can use any type of tape with superior results (even compared to tapes produced with studio machines)			

c

Methodology

Let the S read the phrases on page 52 to help them express their views, so that variations suggested can be properly discussed as in the example given.

Key 🗝 *Key* 🗝 *Key* 🗝 *Key* 🗝

(Suggestions)

Student A: "I can't agree there. If we produced a lean product version of the video recorder with only the essential product features of the original model, we could sell it at a very competitive price."

Student B: "I see things a bit differently. From my point of view we shouldn't try to strip the original model down to its essential features just to make it a bit cheaper. Why don't we have the original model manufactured in the Far East? This would allow us to offer a state-of-the-art product at a really attractive price, which would make it interesting for other markets as well."

Student A: "That's a good point. And as the lower price makes it attractive for a wider market, we could extend our advertising to consumer magazines, household magazines or even TV spots."

Student B: "Exactly. I don't have the slightest doubt …"

**Case study 2:
Wunder power showers**

Methodology

The T should revise possibilities of expressing cause and effect and purpose to help the S vary vocabulary when doing this exercise. Some possibilities are *as, since, due to, so that, in order to, owing to,* etc.

Key 🗝 *Key* 🗝 *Key* 🗝 *Key* 🗝

Wunder has decided to launch its products in Britain, because more British people live in their own homes than Germans. The launch is also due to the fact that only 50% of all British households have a shower. Moreover, the British like to buy more expensive high-performance showers when replacing their old showers so that a shower manufacturer like Wunder is easily attracted to this market. Finally Great Britain is also attractive, since showers are not mainly bought on price.

**B
Product information**

> | i |
>
> Before the S can fully understand the marketing mix decisions for Wunder showers, they need to understand about the product lines available on the market and their use. Note that power showers play an ever increasing role in Great Britain, since the water pressure in many areas is felt to be inadequate for a refreshing shower.

| a |

Key 🗝 *Key* 🗝 *Key* 🗝 *Key* 🗝
1. electric showers
2. mixer showers (thermostatically controlled)
3. mixer showers (manually controlled)
4. power showers

| b |

Key 🗝 *Key* 🗝 *Key* 🗝 *Key* 🗝
(Suggestions)

The new Projet shower is a state-of-the-art shower. It has been fully redeveloped in comparison to its predecessor. The difference between the new Projet and the old model is the Jetclean technology we have built in, the big advantage being a guaranteed continuous forceful needle spray without any lime scale build-up.

Two other major product features are the reduction in weight and the shower's user-friendliness. The Projet is also ahead of its competition, as it can be fitted with our water saving Ecoplus adapter. Last but not least, we give a full five-year guarantee.

In brief one can say that this wall-mounted single-lever shower is the most economical all-purpose shower for instantaneous water heaters or stored hot water systems on the market today.

| c |

Methodology

It would be a good idea to ask the S to do this exercise at home so they can bring along some brochures or overhead transparencies for their product presentations from their companies (or any other favourite products) to make the presentation more lively. If the S don't name the product in the presentation the rest of the class could start a guessing game. The T should allow the description of imaginary products, too, as long as the phrases for describing products are applied correctly.

**C

1 The marketing mix**

Methodology

Depending on the class, the S could be allowed to look up the tapescript for help while listening to the cassette.

| a |

Key 🗝 *Key* 🗝 *Key* 🗝 *Key* 🗝
1. True
2. False. The water flow of electric showers is too weak.
3. True
4. True
5. True.
6. False. They will concentrate on England.

| b |

Key 🗝 *Key* 🗝 *Key* 🗝 *Key* 🗝
product:

Mixer showers will be introduced to cover the market for all-round competitively priced showers. Power showers will cater for the needs of the shower users, who put greater emphasis on a really strong flow of water.

price:

There are two options here:
a) market oriented pricing undercutting the competition to gain market share quickly. This approach is favoured by the Wunder Marketing Director.
b) pricing at the going rate, i.e. charging a similar price to that of the main competitors. Non-price features of the product should be stressed to build up brand character and brand loyalty.

No agreement is found and a decision will be taken the following week.

distribution (place):

see example

advertising (promotion):

Supersite posters, local radio and print ads in household magazines will be used.
Brochures, leaflets, point-of-sale displays and in-store demonstrations, stands at fairs and exhibitions and cash incentives for retailers are the promotion measures considered.

Key 🗝 Key 🗝 Key 🗝 Key 🗝

(See page 56 (CB) for the beginning and the end of the meeting report.)

2. Distribution

They were in full agreement to bypass the wholesale business and to concentrate on big retail outlets for the year of the launch. Later, specialist shops like bathroom shops and builders would be included as well.

3. Pricing

Whereas Wunder management supported market-oriented pricing, thereby undercutting the competition to gain a market share more quickly, the agency advised Wunder to price products at the going rate. This strategy involved stressing non-price features of the product to build up brand character and brand loyalty.

Next steps:
* Finalising pricing policy with Wunder's Marketing Director, Ralph Summers – Yellowhammer – before 14th Sept.

4. Advertising

Supersite posters complemented by local radio and print ads in household magazines were considered appropriate for the launch in terms of timing, coverage, impact and frequency, with the launch area being restricted to England.

5. Sales promotion

Brochures, leaflets, point of sale displays and in-store demonstrations, stands at fairs and exhibitions, cash incentives for retailers and the acquisition of shelf space were considered, but should be more fully discussed at the next meeting.

Next steps:
* Faxing preliminary media plan incl. cinema spots to Wunder – Yellowhammer – before 21st Sept.

Additional exercise

A word family exercise might be added here (verb, noun, person, adjective). Some suitable words from the tapescript include: research, satisfied, segment, performance, retail, price, brand, extension, trade, penetrate, competitor, decide, budget, afford, impact, coverage, promotion, display.
Make sure the S use these in an appropriate context.

---

2 Market research / Folie

Methodology

In order to become familiar with the terms and phrases related to graphs, the S should be asked to describe a variety of graphs and diagrams provided either by the T or the S themselves. Once the S have mastered this activity and done exercises **a** and **b**, the T could produce additional sets of graphs. Only this time the T should provide explanations for certain developments of the graph, which the S will have to incorporate in their descriptions. Moreover, ask the S to vary the link words in their descriptions, paying special attention to sequencing, forecasting, expressing similarity and cause, effect and purpose.
For S with grammar deficiencies, it might be a good idea to revise the present perfect and future tenses (continuous and simple) to help them cope with describing time relationships in graphs.

a
Key 🗝 Key 🗝 Key 🗝 Key 🗝

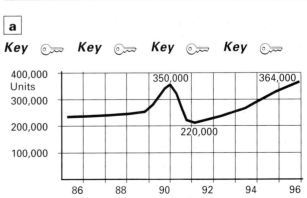

b

Key 🗝 *Key* 🗝 *Key* 🗝 *Key* 🗝

... I'm now going to describe the present market shares (chart 1) and the development of sales on the market for shower systems from 1996 to 2006 (chart 2).

Chart 1 shows that at present the UK market is dominated by four producers, Aqua, Team, Young Shower and Mica, with Mica being the clear market leader. Their market share amounts to 34%, whereas the market share of the remaining competitors takes up between 13% and 17%, totalling 63%. Other producers make up 17%; the market share of Trenton stands at a negligible 3%.

Let us now turn to chart 2. Here you can see that shower sales rose constantly from £150m in 1996 to a peak of over £220m in 1999. The decline to £180m over the last year has been a result of the general recession in the European economy. However, with our promising outlook for the future, I am absolutely confident that sales will pick up considerably, increasing to £280m in 2005. After that the completion of more and more new housing estates should even produce a dramatic increase in shower sales.

Concluding, one can say that there has been and that there still is an underlying upward trend in the British shower market, which ought to guarantee a successful market entry for Wunder. Have you got any questions?

c

Key 🗝 *Key* 🗝 *Key* 🗝 *Key* 🗝

TV set with VCR
a slide projector
a marker
OHP pens
an overhead projector
a tape recorder
a computer with a CD ROM drive, 3.5" disk drive
a CD ROM
a flip chart
a whiteboard
a screen

D Phone calls:
A telephone interview

Methodology

In more advanced groups exercise **a** and **b** might be done together, with the second listening concentrating on the language aspect of exercise **c** (the polite formula).

a

Key 🗝 *Key* 🗝 *Key* 🗝 *Key* 🗝

1. Introduction
2. Personal data of interviewee
3. Information on product (shower) in use
3.1 Make
3.2 Time in use
3.3 Reason(s) for buying a shower
3.4 Point of purchase
3.5 Disadvantages of present model
3.6 Strong points of shower
4. Qualities of an ideal shower
5. Attitudes towards shower advertising

b

Key 🗝 *Key* 🗝 *Key* 🗝 *Key* 🗝

1. Introduction
The interviewer introduces her company, Yellowhammer Research Services, and the product range they want to get people's opinions on, i.e. showers.

2. Personal data of interviewee
2.1 Name: Midwinter, Mr
2.2 Occupation: full time house-husband
2.3 Wife's occupation: lawyer
3. Information on product in use
3.1 Make: Ricon Y 99
3.2 Time in use: 7 years
3.3 Reason(s) for buying a shower: to save money on hot water bills
3.4 Point of purchase: DIY shop
3.5 Disadvantages of present model:
　* weak flow of water with high temperatures
　* low temperatures with strong flows
　* temperature not kept up continuously
　* lime scale build-up in shower head, which needs to be taken apart frequently
3.6 Strong points of shower: none
4. Qualities of an ideal shower:
　* strong flow of water whatever the temperature of the water
　* value for money
　* reasonably-sized showerhead
　* functional design
5. Attitudes towards shower advertising
　* bathrooms shown look sterile and costly
　* ads are uninteresting, dull and uninformative regarding price
　* there is too much bare female skin shown

c

Key 🗝 *Key* 🗝 *Key* 🗝 *Key* 🗝

– Do you have a few moments to spare?
– ..., please?
– Could you tell me ...?
– Could you be more specific?

- What else would you say ...?
- Perhaps you could (explain) ...?
- May I (note)...?
- What do you think are ...?

Methodology

The T should provide the S with either a labelled drawing of a car or with a word list to help them with some of the more difficult technical vocabulary. (See also CB, page 36) A German-English dictionary might also help. Consider the possibility of group interviews with two interviewees to an interviewer.
Some basic vocabulary:

windscreen – Windschutzscheibe
tank – Tank
speedometer – Geschwindigkeitsmesser/Tachometer
ignition – Zündung
clutch – Kupplung
gear – Gang
change gears – schalten
accelerator (pedal) – Gas (-pedal)
horn – Hupe
radiator – Kühler
bonnet *(Brit.)* – Motorhaube
hood *(Am.)* – Motorhaube
boot *(Brit.)* – Kofferraum
trunk *(Am.)* – Kofferraum
exhaust pipe – Auspuffrohr
headlight – Scheinwerfer
flat tyre/puncture – Platten
fuel consumption – Benzinverbrauch
safety belts – Sicherheitsgurte
storage space – Laderaum

E
Comparing advertisements

Key ⚬⇌ Key ⚬⇌ Key ⚬⇌ Key ⚬⇌

	Aquarius	**British Power**	**Tiger**
1. Product & producer	Aquarius shower range by Aquarius PLC (public limited company)	gas power showers by British Power	full range of showers by Tiger showers
2. Medium	probably household, general interest or women's magazines	see Aquarius	see Aquarius
3. Layout	mint headline with eye-catching imperative (Look), two column body copy (white on blue background), caption/slogan, contact, illustration with insert (control unit)	headline (imperative and colour to flag reader down) with subhead, one column body copy and illustration each taking up almost half of the full page ad, insert sketches of showerhead and controls, logo, slogan/claim	headline, illustration with integrated superimposed benefits and "reason whys", logo and slogan/claim, strapline with range and price information and contact; probably double spread; b/w ad with one additional colour as opposed to other 4 colour ads
4. Illustration	key visual of man showering (red shower attracting attention) with insert of control	waterfall with branches hanging into the water	wall-mounted showerhead with water gushing out and superimposed benefits and "reason whys" (red as an eye catcher in headline, superimposition and claim/slogan)
5. Body copy (heading see illustration)	going straight to the point, concentrating on product attributes expressed by nouns, adjectives and an intensifying adverb all with positive connotations; simple syntax and repetitive vocabulary	body copy starts from major problems generally associated with electric showers (changing water temperature & low pressure) and then presents the gas power shower as the solution; it implicitly criticises electric showers (Unlike the standard electric showers, our ...); frequently the reader is addressed personally (you) like in a sales talk	no body copy, but a range of benefits and "reason whys" integrated in the illustration

	Aquarius	British Power	Tiger
6. Benefits – rational	wide product range, ease of installation and use, safety, high performance, reliability, (popularity)	powerful jets, steady temperature at all times, variable spray patterns, easy fit, good value for money	more power, more performance, better design, adjustable spray handsets, easy installation
– emotional	attractive styling, popularity	refreshing & strong like a waterfall	you get more (performance, value for your money etc.)
7. Reason Why	testimonial (Britain's most popular shower)	price quoted (from £289), fitted booster pump, adjustable nozzle; illustration supports emotional reason why	better design, better engineering, state-of-the-art technology, adjustable spray handsets
8. Slogan	Refreshingly fine showers (emphasis on quality and design)	Showers are our business (emphasis on competence)	The showers of the Future (emphasis on advanced technology)
9. Tonality – atmosphere	light, clean, refreshing	powerful, forceful, refreshing, natural	concentration on shower power
– style	informative	formal, informative, rational	catchwords, less informative
10. Target group all ads: – home owners – flat owners – handy men – (mainly men)	conservative users (as the ad is very traditional) with lower and middle income, demanding average quality (although the range is wide)	users with gas heating and middle/higher income, who demand a higher quality	probably younger users with middle income
11. Strengths and weaknesses *Please note that strengths and weaknesses of an ad can only be judged by considering the target group the ad aims at. An apparently bad ad may turn out to be just the right thing for a particular target group.*	points for discussion: – too many benefits, no USP – unattractive shower decor – tonality comes across as somewhat sterile and bland	points for discussion: – body copy too rational (no shower experience as promised in illustration and headline) + more clearly defined target group	points for discussion: + unusual concept for attracting attention – layout and colour scheme make it difficult for the reader to see the benefits and "reason whys" presented; benefits and "reason whys" are therefore lost) – tonality somewhat sterile (but is probably intended to be so)

b

Key *Key* *Key* *Key*

1. ad under a particular heading (like cars for sale etc.)
2. poster site, usually at roadside
3. net sale of a publication (less than readership)
4. tunes with slogans/claims used in TV and radio commercials
5. exaggeration used in advertising
6. advertising at product introduction
7. statement usually by product users (frequently VIPs) endorsing the product
8. marketing a product or service by phone
9. gift used in direct response marketing
10. total annual turnover of an advertising agency

c

Methodology

If possible, the S should bring some advertising material either from the companies where they are working or taken from newspapers etc. for discussion and comparison.

UNIT 5
Complaints and adjustments

Contents/Targets

Unit 5 concentrates on difficulties in fulfilling the contract of sale. It not only deals with delays in delivery and payment but also shows how a faulty delivery is handled. The unit is rounded off with the mention of some essential laws protecting consumers.

Starter: Here, a cartoon is presented showing a car that has just lost a wheel roaring down a sloping road.

A: The way in which a particular supplier deals with complaints is shown here.

B: By writing commercial letters and listening to a dialogue, the S learn how to deal with delays in delivery.

C: The S learn how to cope with a damaged consignment.

D: Here, the S get to know ways in which to handle a delay in payment.

E: In this section, the S learn about consumer protection from a text illustrating, in extracts, the most important laws.

Starter

Key ⚷ *Key* ⚷ *Key* ⚷ *Key* ⚷

a

The purpose of a cartoon is of course to exaggerate but without losing the awareness of the essentials. Here, the cartoonist either wants to point out that someone has forgotten to bolt the wheel tight in a garage or that a manufacturing fault might have produced this incident.

b

Depending on the answer of **a** either the mechanic or the supplier/producer is to blame.

The answer centres on a manufacturing fault. The producer could take back the new car and replace it, or he could arrange the repair of the car if it makes any sense. But, whichever solution the manufacturer offers, he should apologize.

- damage to the paintwork/body
- defects of the engine, gearbox etc.
- problems with the electronics
- delay in delivery etc.

Possible solutions: replacement or repair depending on the extent of the damage, withdrawal from the contract or reduction in price

A
Dealing with complaints

Methodology:

Before starting with the text, the S could give examples of how their companies react when dealing with complaints.

a

Key ⚷ *Key* ⚷ *Key* ⚷ *Key* ⚷

1. available
2. check
3. treat
4. thoroughly
5. uncertain
6. error
7. defective
8. complex

b

Key ⚷ *Key* ⚷ *Key* ⚷ *Key* ⚷

1. Possible reasons: delay in delivery or payment/defective goods/incomplete consignment/goods are not the quality ordered/wrong goods are delivered
2. Politeness is a feature of business culture that always helps to ease interpersonal relations.
3. Without checking the reasons for a complaint, a possible error or defective goods may be noticed too late, resulting in more and more dissatisfied customers complaining.
4. Possible solutions: replacement/repair/reduction in price/release from the contract
5. The customer is not interested in a complex explanation, he wants the matter settled as quickly as possible. Blaming the staff means admitting that the company's personnel is not competent, which may ruin the company's reputation. Furthermore, the staff will be frustrated and unmotivated.
6. A thorough check can avoid possible further complaints.
7. On the one hand this shows a certain kind of responsibility, making sure the customers will not lose their confidence in the company; on the other hand, if greater damage can be averted this way, it may save the company a lot of money, e.g. for compensation claims.
8. It has become common practice for car manufacturers to call back certain models in order to replace defective parts.

Unit 5 · 31

c

Key 🗝 *Key* 🗝 *Key* 🗝 *Key* 🗝

The answers depend on the S' own experience. Here, the main emphasis is put on the differences compared to the examples in the book.

B
Delay in delivery

> *i*
>
> In this part of the unit the S should understand that delays in delivery constitute a breach of contract caused by the supplier, unless they are due to force majeure (strike, flood, earthquake etc.).
> The customer has got the right to claim compensation from the supplier for the losses sustained by him, if the supplier is not able to carry out his part of the contract. Very often the parties agree on a compensation payable in the event of a breach of contract by either party.

a

Methodology
The S should study the letter first before completing it.

Key 🗝 *Key* 🗝 *Key* 🗝 *Key* 🗝

1. received
2. extremely
3. consignment
4. in time
5. apologies
6. production line
7. face *(v.)*
8. sorted out
9. cleared up
10. according to
11. inconvenience
12. rely on

b

Methodology
The S should be allowed to use a dictionary if necessary.
The T should remind the S to write a complete letter containing all necessary elements, like address, subject line, etc. Any missing details should be invented. As it is an answer letter, the S should invent a name (Dear Mr …/Ms …).

Key 🗝 *Key* 🗝 *Key* 🗝 *Key* 🗝

Model letter:

> Wolf GmbH
> Rosenheimer Straße 156
> D–80147 München
> Tel.: 089/62 13-24 71
> Fax: 089/62 13-39 60
>
> India Electronics Ltd.
> 112 Connought Road
> New Delhi 110055
> India
>   7 March, …
>
> **Consignment (No. …) of electronic parts**
>
> Dear Mr Birendra,
>
> We have received your letter of … and we apologize for the delay, which is due to a serious breakdown in our production department.
> We will, however, be able to deliver the goods ordered in two weeks' time.
> We are sorry about the inconvenience this has caused you.
>
> Yours sincerely,

c

Methodology
After having answered a letter of complaint, the S should write a letter of complaint now, again using the phrases from the box.
As the Canadian supplier has always delivered on time up to now, it makes more sense for the writer of the letter to use a rather mild tone here. As it is a well known-customer, the S should invent a name (Dear Mr …/Ms …) rather than start the letter with "Dear Sirs/Dear Sir or Madam".

Key 🗝 *Key* 🗝 *Key* 🗝 *Key* 🗝

Model letter:

> **Möbeldesign GmbH**
> Wesselinger Straße 11
> D–50342 Köln
> Tel.: 0221/53 44 70
> Fax: 0221/53 44 75
>
> Woodpecker Ltd.
> 108 Commander Boulevard
> Agincourt
> M1S 3C7 Ontario
> Canada
>
> 18 August, ...
>
> Dear Mr ... /Ms ...
>
> We regret to inform you that our order No. XYZ is overdue. The consignment of hardwood was promised to arrive here in Cologne before 5 August.
>
> As it is now 18 August, we would appreciate it if you could dispatch it within the next ten days.
>
> Yours sincerely,

d

Methodology

Here, the S do not only listen for gist but also for some details.

Key 🗝 *Key* 🗝 *Key* 🗝 *Key* 🗝

Colin and John are talking about an overdue consignment of urgently-needed batteries. The problem has been caused by an unexpected rise in demand for these batteries. They are planning to send a fax, in which the supplier is asked to deliver the goods by Wednesday at the latest, otherwise they would hold the supplier responsible for the loss and claim compensation from them.

e

Key 🗝 *Key* 🗝 *Key* 🗝 *Key* 🗝

1. Due to an unexpected rise in demand for the batteries, Hartmann had delivery problems.
2. Manson & Attkins (M & A) themselves would get into trouble with regard to their customers.
3. Because other suppliers could not deliver in time either.
4. Compensation for the loss could be claimed.

f

Methodology

Here, groups of S should work out a dialogue using the prompts. After that, one or two pairs could role-play the situation. The S should invent any missing details.

Key 🗝 *Key* 🗝 *Key* 🗝 *Key* 🗝

Model dialogue:

Student A
(Purchasing Manager)

Student B
(representative)

> ..., guten Morgen.

> Good morning, this is ... of Smother's Ltd. We'd like to complain about a delay in delivery. A consignment of 1,000 wheels has been now overdue for two months.

> Oh, I'm very sorry, Mr ... Could you please tell me the order No.?

Unit 5 · 33

Yes, certainly. It's W 89701.

Well, let me see. Ah, here we are. It was for 1,000 wheels for your *Fun Trek bikes*.

That's right. Could you tell me why there's such a delay on this order? Our customers are already very annoyed.

Yes, I understand that. Unfortunately there was a fire in our production plant and we couldn't find another supplier in such a short time.

Oh, I'm sorry to hear that, but time is pressing now. Our customers are waiting for the new line.

Well, we've resumed production now and as we'll give your order priority, we should be able to deliver within 7 days. Will that be all right?

I think one week should be OK, but I hope that such a long delay will not happen again.

Well, we always do our best to deliver on time, but an accident like a fire is beyond our control.

I know that you've always been a reliable supplier and I'm glad that this matter is settled now. I'll be in touch when your consignment arrives. Thank you for your help. Bye.

Goodbye, Mr ...

C
Faulty delivery

> *i*
>
> The supplier is obliged to deliver the goods without damage.
> Should the goods be defective or faulty, they are placed at the supplier's disposal.
> In case of only minor defects, the customer will probably keep the goods, but can claim an allowance (reduction in price).
> In many other cases, faulty goods can be repaired or must be replaced.

a

Key ⚷ *Key* ⚷ *Key* ⚷ *Key* ⚷

Model letter:

Dear Mr Möbius,

We received your letter of ... and the damaged switches today.

We are really sorry to hear that the consignment arrived in a bad condition.

As we pursue a philosophy of high standard quality, we have investigated the matter thoroughly and found out that the plating was not thick enough. That's why some of the switches had scratches.

Please accept our apologies for the inconvenience caused by this fault in workmanship.

We are certainly prepared to replace the defective goods as soon as possible.

We assure you that there will be no further cause to complain.

Yours sincerely,

b

Key 🗝 *Key* 🗝 *Key* 🗝 *Key* 🗝

Model letter:

Dear Sir or Madam (Dear Sirs),

The shipment ordered on 10 April finally arrived here today.
We are sorry to inform you that we are highly dissatisfied with the execution of the order. Firstly, you failed to keep to the delivery period of four weeks stated in your acknowledgement for the 24 swivel towel holders ordered, so that we were forced to send you two reminders in the meantime.
Secondly, the shipment does not meet the quality ordered. Instead of brass the towel holders are chromium plated.
As our hotel will be reopened on 15 June after the renovation, we are in serious doubts whether we can keep the date at all. That is why we will reserve the right to claim compensation from you for the delay, should you not manage to deliver the towel holders by 10 June.

Yours faithfully,
Günter Möbius
Managing Director
Hotel Scandinavia

c

Key 🗝 *Key* 🗝 *Key* 🗝 *Key* 🗝

1. a replacement is most sensible
2. a replacement or repair seems to be most adequate
3. either replacement or a reduction in price if the furniture can be sold

D
Delay in payment

> *i*
>
> If an invoice is overlooked by the customer, or if he fails to pay within the credit period granted, delays in payment will occur.
> It is a case of non-payment if the customer is in a state of insolvency (Zahlungsunfähigkeit). Very often, legal steps are taken as a last resort. When an account becomes overdue, the supplier should inform the customer either by telephone, a copy of the invoice, or a letter. These are called reminders. If the first reminder is not satisfactory, it is followed, as a rule, by two (or more) collection letters that are graded in tone. That means that the request for payment becomes more and more insistent and urgent.

1. Reminders

a

Methodology

As the two companies have already had business connections for some time, it wouldn't make any sense to start the letter with „Dear Sirs". The S should therefore invent a name and start the opening salutation with „Dear Mr ... or Dear Ms ... The S should also invent other missing details (address, telephone numbers, etc.).

Key 🗝 *Key* 🗝 *Key* 🗝 *Key* 🗝

Model letter:

Dear Mr ... / Ms ...,

We wrote to you on ... asking for payment of the overdue invoice No. B 876312 for £ 2,160. We are surprised that you have not paid the last invoice up to now, as you always settled your former accounts promptly. We need the amount urgently, because we have to pay our supplier. We would expect payment by ... at the latest. As we have had good business relations with you so far, we trust that it is only an error and that you will settle the invoice within the period stipulated.

Yours sincerely,

b

Key 🗝 *Key* 🗝 *Key* 🗝 *Key* 🗝

As a delay in payment is not Greenwood's usual business habit, Mr Jones suggests a careful treatment of this matter.

c

Key 🗝 *Key* 🗝 *Key* 🗝 *Key* 🗝

1. She notices it from the morning's computer print-outs.
2. Greenwood's account shows a debit balance of £ 5,000.
3. She has sent them a copy of the invoice.
4. In the case of McDouglas Truck Inc. three collection letters had to be sent after the first application for payment.

2. Phone calls:
reminding customers on the phone

a

Key 🗝 *Key* 🗝 *Key* 🗝 *Key* 🗝

As the S should learn to be especially polite when dealing with long-standing customers – otherwise they would run the risk of losing them – the following phrases should be avoided:
I've got a serious complaint.

It's definitely your fault.
We must insist on prompt payment.

b

Key ⚯ ***Key*** ⚯ ***Key*** ⚯ ***Key*** ⚯

Possible further answers could be: I'll check it with .../I'm awfully sorry, but at the moment the file is not available./Mr/Ms ... is not in at the moment, but he/she'll phone you later./I'm sure we have already settled the account but nevertheless I'll check it.

c

Key ⚯ ***Key*** ⚯ ***Key*** ⚯ ***Key*** ⚯

Model dialogue:

Student A

Good morning. John Black of White & Co. speaking. I'd like to speak to Mr Gordon of the Purchasing Department, please.

Hello, Paul, this is John Black speaking. I'm phoning about your invoice No. 324 for lighting fittings.

It may have slipped your mind that your invoice was due on 12 September, but it is still outstanding.

Student B
Switchboard:

Beta Ltd, good morning.

Just a minute, I'll put you through.

Paul Gordon speaking.

Hello, John, please wait a moment, I'll just get the file. – Okay, where seems to be the problem?

Oh yes, you're quite right there, and I was absolutely sure we had settled the account in time. Mr Ballantine is in charge of the invoicing department, I'm afraid he isn't in today. I'll tell him first thing tomorrow and he'll phone you immediately.

Thank you very much, Paul. But please see to it that it is settled within the next few days at the latest, because it is already three weeks overdue.

Of course, John. And I apologize for any inconvenience caused by our oversight.

d

Key ⚯ ***Key*** ⚯ ***Key*** ⚯ ***Key*** ⚯

The answer depends on the S' own experience.

E
Consumer protection

> *i*
>
> The consumer can quite rightly expect to receive goods and services that not only match their descriptions, but are not faulty, dangerous or unfit for use. Over the years, the law has developed guidelines for all kinds of transactions to provide a means of dealing with disputes between supplier and consumer.
> Furthermore, the law tries to address the imbalance between the power of a large organisation, which will have the backing of specialists and lawyers, and the vulnerability of the individual consumer.

Methodology

The S should look up unknown words in their dictionaries.

Key ⚯ ***Key*** ⚯ ***Key*** ⚯ ***Key*** ⚯

1. false
2. true
3. false
4. false
5. false

Unit 6
Modes of payment

Contents / Targets

This unit deals with modes and types of payment, especially from and to other countries, giving some insight into reasons why these modes are used. Business insurance is also touched upon.

Starter: Here, different modes of payment are shown.

A: Types of payment are compared along with their applications, and some types of export payment are documented: the Bill of Exchange (B/E), Documents against Payment (D/P), Documents against Acceptance (D/A), and the Letter of Credit (L/C).

B: The S learn how to negotiate and compare the different modes of payment, and how to choose the most suitable one for the situation. The S.W.I.F.T. system is shown and explained.

C: Part C is an introduction into electronic banking.

D: Here, the S learn how to negotiate discounts and modes of payment and how to enquire about insurance on the phone.

E: The insurance of foreign trade transactions, a very important factor for all exporters, is explained here.

Starter

Methodology

The T may ask the S to name the modes of payment shown here (Vocabulary: US Dollars, coins [small change], notes, credit cards, pay-in slip).

A

1 Comparing types of payment

Methodology

The S should study the table on the different types of payment before doing exercise **a**.

a

Key *Key* *Key* *Key*

1. Direct debiting
2. Standing order
3. Letter of credit
4. Credit card, cash
5. Bill of exchange

b

Key *Key* *Key* *Key*

"Laundering money" means transferring the proceeds of illegal transactions (e.g. payment for armaments, drug profits) to a bank in another country, where the money is then invested, changed to another currency or simply re-transferred through some other banks to the original sender's account. The money is then "clean", i.e., nobody can trace its origin.

2 The Bill of Exchange (B/E) *Bankwechsel*

a

A Bill of Exchange is a document issued by a seller and signed by a purchaser, stating that the purchaser accepts that he owes the seller money, and promises to pay it at a later date. The person issuing the bill is the drawer, the person who accepts it is the drawee. The seller can then sell the bill at a discount to raise cash. This is called a "trade bill". A bill can also be accepted (i.e. guaranteed) by a bank, and in this case it is called a "bank bill".

(PONS-Fachwörterbuch Bank- und Finanzwesen, Ernst Klett Verlag 1993, ISBN 3-12-517840)

D/P (Documents against Payment) – this is when the shipping documents, without which the importer cannot collect his consignment from the ship, are handed over by the importer's bank when payment is made.

D/A (Documents against Acceptance) – here, the shipping documents are handed over when the importer signs (accepts) the B/E. After that, it is the responsibility of the banks to see that the exporter gets his money. *ok*

I

Key *Key* *Key* *Key*

E, C, D, B, F, A

II

Key *Key* *Key* *Key*

E, C, D, A, F, B

Unit 6 · 37

b

Key 🔑 ***Key*** 🔑 ***Key*** 🔑 ***Key*** 🔑

The main difference is that in D/P, the payment takes place on presentation of the documents (with the B/E, this is a sight bill), while with D/A, the bank (and the exporter) extends credit to the importer until the date of maturity of the bill (a time bill).

3 Issuing a documentary Akkreditiv Letter of Credit (L/C)

i

The L/C is a bank guarantee which ensures that the seller will receive payment. The buyer opens a separate account at his bank, from which the payment for the imported goods will be made. Money from this account may not be withdrawn during the period of currency of the L/C. Thus, the opener of the L/C cannot change his mind and try to get his money back when the goods are already being produced or even on their way to him. On the other hand, he gets interest on the money, because it is *his* bank account. When the goods arrive, have been inspected by "Norske Veritas" (see page 86, CB), and are found to be in order, he instructs his bank to release the payment if the goods have been delivered within the time limit, in the correct way, and without any cause for complaint.

Key 🔑 ***Key*** 🔑 ***Key*** 🔑 ***Key*** 🔑

1. contract
2. exporter
3. issuing
4. beneficiary
5. shipping documents
6. advising
7. order
8. repayment
9. debiting
10. port
11. issuing

B

1 Payments from abroad

a

Key 🔑 ***Key*** 🔑 ***Key*** 🔑 ***Key*** 🔑

1. in cash
2. in advance
3. cheque
4. B/E or L/C
5. L/C or B/E
6. cheque
7. B/E
8. L/C
9. cheque
10. account
11. B/E
12. L/C

b

Key 🔑 ***Key*** 🔑 ***Key*** 🔑 ***Key*** 🔑

1. reputation
2. in advance
3. taking into consideration
4. buy in bulk
5. wholesalers
6. unprofitable

c

Key 🔑 ***Key*** 🔑 ***Key*** 🔑 ***Key*** 🔑

1. As the agencies usually charge their own commissions, it may be more profitable for a company to sell their goods directly. Furthermore, agencies often have their own advertising guidelines, which may not be suitable for the producer's products.
2. At trade fairs, the company has the chance of meeting buyers from all parts of the world. These buyers will be importers, not private persons, and thus the company's sales chances will be improved.
3. Money in the form of cash is normally very difficult to trace. It is thus ideal for making illegal payments. In some countries (e.g. the USA) persons paying cash may be looked upon as suspicious.
4. A B/E is a promise to pay. Normally, by the time a B/E reaches the drawee, the goods have been produced. If the drawee refuses to pay, the drawer is left with goods on his hands which he probably can't get rid of without losing money.
5. Seller: By receiving cash in advance, he has obliged himself to fulfil the contract under all circumstances.
   Buyer: He cannot work with the money in the meantime (no interest, no chance of short-term investment).

d

Methodology

The T is recommended to read the details on the Letter of Credit before attempting this exercise with the S.

Key 🔑 ***Key*** 🔑 ***Key*** 🔑 ***Key*** 🔑
(Suggestions)

1. Sight bill. He has good references, and wants to buy in bulk. This could be your great chance.
2. Payment by cheque or time bill – by the time the cheque is cleared or the bill is at maturity, the customer will have had plenty of use out of the money. Another point here is that if the customer buys later, the price of the samples might be deducted from his final invoice. This is effective in getting orders, but depends, of course, on the value of the samples.

3. In this case, the safest method is cash in advance or a letter of credit. Otherwise it is advisable to get an export credit guarantee (see page 91 in the CB).
4. The most suitable method of payment here is the (confirmed) letter of credit (irrevocable) against shipping documents. If it is confirmed, the confirming bank is responsible for the payment. If it is irrevocable, the customer cannot change his/her mind at the last minute. When the L/C is against shipping documents, the issuing bank arranges transfer of the payment, not the customer. An export credit guarantee is also advisable (see page 91 in the CB).

e

Key Key Key Key
A 6-month B/E means that the company either has to wait 6 months for payment of the time bill, or discount the bill, which still takes time. Also, the customer has to pay discounting charges, which are quite expensive. Instead of that, he might look for a cheaper supplier. Cash in advance would of course be most acceptable, followed by payment on receipt of merchandise. Most firms dealing with large export orders for machines ask for 1/3 payment with order, 1/3 on advice of readiness of shipment, and 1/3 30 days after successful commissioning (after the machines have been running successfully for 30 days at the importer's place of business).

f

Key Key Key Key
The answer depends on the S.

2 A S.W.I.F.T message

b

Key Key Key Key
A – 6, B – 7, C – 1, D – 2, E – 9, F – 8, G – 3, H – 5, I – 10, J – 4

c

Key Key Key Key
1. The date on which the L/C becomes invalid (Ablaufdatum)
2. When a consignment is too large to be sent with one ship, truck, or plane, it is split into the minimum number of partial shipments that may be conveniently transported (Teilsendung).
3. The person receiving the payment (Begünstigter)
4. The document cannot be sold or transferred to any other person or firm (nicht übertragbar).
5. The date on which the bank issues the L/C (Ausstellungsdatum)
6. Sum of money (Betrag)
7. The person who asks for the L/C to be opened (Antragsteller)
8. Bearing the address of (adressiert an)
9. When a ship, truck, or plane does not go the whole distance to the destination, the goods must be unloaded and then reloaded on a further means of transport (Umladung). (Note that the following spelling is also possible: transhipment)
10. To inform (benachrichtigen)
11. Money paid to a middleman for helping to promote business (e.g. finding customers, suppliers, etc. (Provision)
12. Costs incurred at banks, customs, etc. for paperwork (Gebühren)

d

Key Key Key Key
1. A B/E is normally used when the parties to the transaction know each other and the seller is prepared to wait for a limited time for his money (or the buyer is prepared to pay the bank charges for discounting the B/E). Here, the time is too long (9 months), and Keller probably does not know Kinnison & Samms very well.
2. There is no security for Keller this way. On arrival of the goods the customer may turn out to be insolvent.

3 Negotiating terms of payment

a

Key Key Key Key
1. enquiry
2. state
3. well-known
4. D/A
5. cheque
6. COD
7. shipment
8. L/C
9. SWIFT
10. destination

b

Key Key Key Key
Im Großen und Ganzen ist die Firma mit unserem Angebot einverstanden, aber sie akzeptiert nicht die geforderte Zahlung durch Akkreditiv. Greek Trade International verweist auf ihre ausgezeichneten Referenzen. Zudem sei es in der Firma üblich, mit 90 Tage Sichtwechsel zu bezahlen. Sie verweisen darauf, dass sie ihren

Kunden sogar bis zu 240 Tagen Kredit einräumen müssen und bitten uns, unsere Zahlungsbedingungen noch einmal zu überdenken.

c

Key *Key* *Key* *Key*
(Model letter)

Greek Trade International
29 Omonia Square
Athens

4 March, ...

Dear Mr Xanthopoulos,

Your letter of 25 February

We have read your request for different terms of payment with interest. We agree that your references are very good, and we also understand the difficult situation you are faced with in Greece.

As our usual terms for first orders are payment by letter of credit, we cannot but follow our company policy in this matter. We are prepared, however, to make a concession in this case and would suggest offering you 3% discount for payment by L/C at 90 days' sight.

We are certain that our products will meet your expectations and you will find that they have a ready sale with your customers.

We look forward to hearing from you soon.

Yours sincerely,
Karl-Heinz Keller

d

Key *Key* *Key* *Key*
(Model letter)

KERNOW PRINTERS
THE PRINTERS FOR CORNWALL
36 Culdrose St
Lamorna
Cornwall

Illumino Publications,
35 Golden Apple Street
St. Mary's
Scilly Isles

Attn. Mr. H. Celine   23 September 19..

Dear Mr Celine,

Your order for 5 gross 4-colour letterheads

Thank you very much for your letter dated 19 September, 19.. in which you state that your preferred terms of payment are by 90 days' draft.

Unfortunately, since your company is unknown to us, we are not able to grant you these conditions for your first order.

As it is a small order, we would suggest that you place it on a COD basis or pay cash in advance. In the latter case, a discount of 6% and 3% in the former case would be possible.

We trust that you will agree to one of these terms.

Yours sincerely,
R. Wilson

C
Electronic banking

Key *Key* *Key* *Key*

a

The answer depends on the S.

b

1. Administration costs are reduced because of automation. The working capital balance is more efficiently controlled, and cash management thus improved. In addition, the money-transfer time is zero.

2. Electronic Cash is the name used for payment with "plastic money". ATM is the 24-hour "tin teller" (Blechkassierer) where money is available for holders of a valid card.

3. A screen, a modem, and a telephone are necessary. (You must have your PIN as well, but a number isn't a device – be sure to remind the S of this.)

4. Advantages: The lack of time delay coupled with the ability to send communications with the transfer (EDIFACT), the fact that there is no need to carry cash, the availability of money and account information 24 hours a day (ATM), the fact that you have the bank at home (home banking), and the possibility of having an instant check of a company's finances.
   Disadvantages: The automation reduces the workforce necessary (unemployment and redundancy), the risk of theft of cheque and eurocards, and the risk of errors (no person to help you or point out any mistake you may have made).

D

1 Phone calls: Negotiating discounts and modes of payment

a

Key 🗝 *Key* 🗝 *Key* 🗝 *Key* 🗝

Hans Sieper bedankt sich für die Anfrage Roderick Graemes bezüglich Scheren und Zubehör. Er informiert Herrn Graeme darüber, dass er ihm einen Katalog zugeschickt hat.
Herr Graeme erwidert, dass er bereits einen guten Überblick über die Produkte der Firma habe und dass er sich für 15.000 Spezialscheren für Elektronikläden und für 20.000 chirurgische Scheren interessiere. Hans Sieper bietet ihm einen Rabatt von 12% an, Herr Graeme möchte einen Rabatt von 18% und man einigt sich schließlich auf einen Rabatt von 15%, wobei Herr Graeme aber Unterstützung bei der Werbung erwartet. Bei der Zahlung einigt man sich nach kurzer Verhandlung auf einen 90-Tage Sichtwechsel.
Die beiden schließen das Gespräch mit einer Verabredung auf der Interelektronika-Messe in Prag.

b

Key 🗝 *Key* 🗝 *Key* 🗝 *Key* 🗝

1. He is interested in scissors and accessories (15,000 special scissors for electronic stores and 20,000 surgical scissors).
2. They finally agree on a 15% discount.
3. It is a draft at 90 days' sight, including bank charges and discounting fees.
4. He wants to have some help with the advertising, as well.

c

(Model dialogue)

Is that Roderick Graeme?

> Yes, speaking.

You remember you faxed us the confirmation of our order for various types of scissors yesterday?

> Yes, I faxed it yesterday morning.

I've just looked through it and there seems to have been some kind of a misunderstanding.

> Just a minute, I'll get our copy.
> Here it is.

If you look at page 2, you'll see there's been a mistake.

> Whereabouts is it on the page?

It's about the middle. Didn't we say 90 days' sight on the phone? (Wasn't our agreement 90 days' sight?)

> Yes. That's right. Let me see ...
> Oh, I really must apologize. My secretary must have looked at my old notes – from before the call – reading 60 days' sight.

Could you send us the correct confirmation as soon as possible?

> Of course. I'll have the correction faxed to you immediately. This will definitely be the correct offer.

Fine. I'll need it urgently for the bank.

> I'd like to apologize again for the inconvenience we've caused you. How about a really good dinner on the last day of the Interelektronika? I know a little restaurant in Prague that's really something.

Oh, that sounds promising.
See you in Prague then.

> I look forward to it.
> Goodbye.

2 Phone calls: Enquiring about an insurance

a

Key 🗝 *Key* 🗝 *Key* 🗝 *Key* 🗝

Mr Beckmann, from Keller KG, wants some information about insurance for an export consignment worth more than 375,000 marks. He explains details of the shipment and the Insurance Representative asks when, how, and to whom, etc. it will go.
Mr Beckmann explains that it's not all finalised yet, and the Insurance Representative asks for details 3 weeks in advance.
Mr Beckmann promises to fax them through. He also explains why he chose this forwarding agent: They were recommended to Keller KG.

b

Key 🗝 *Key* 🗝 *Key* 🗝 *Key* 🗝

The following information is needed: date of shipment, destination, means of shipment, contents, and whether transshipment or partial shipments are permitted.

c

Key 🗝 *Key* 🗝 *Key* 🗝 *Key* 🗝

The answer depends on the S, but standard precautions are to find out what reputation and experience the insurance company has, and whether it is able/allowed to offer this type of insurance (for example, certain Middle-East countries only allow insurance by a domestic company). Important factors are, again, the reputation, experience, ability and permission (as above), and the price.

E
The export credit guarantee

Key 🗝 *Key* 🗝 *Key* 🗝 *Key* 🗝

1. This is offering the goods to a group of people/companies, and allowing these to make bids. The highest bidder receives the goods.
2. No. Big companies have risks that are just as great, if not greater.
3. The new government might have no money left after taking over from the old one. Without money, a government can cancel a project and declare a moratorium on its own debts to other countries.
4. No, but closely connected with their respective governments.
5. The usual reason is that a government is more likely than a private person or firm to have some property in the country of the insurance company. It is thus easier to seize this property and get some of the money back.
6. This will, of course, improve the balance of trade, since it means that the exporter can offer his goods at lower prices This in turn means that more foreign currency will enter the country.
7. Democratic governments must not help any one private individual more than any other. If the government grants insurance to some companies, it will have to grant insurance to all companies.

Unit 7
Transport

Contents/Targets

This unit looks at various aspects of transport. After a comparison of the different modes of transport available the unit concentrates on the dealings of Transglobe, an English Freight Forwarder who is making inroads into the German transport market and dealing with several German companies requiring transport services and advice.

Starter: Photos of rail, road, sea and air transport serve as an introduction into the subject matter.

A: The S are presented with a table that compares air and sea transport for a shipment from Hamburg to South Africa. Having compared these two modes on the basis of the data provided, other modes of transport, i.e. rail and road are compared. The S are then asked to role-play a first conversation between a freight forwarding company and a customer based on the table.

B: The S get acquainted with the range of services provided by a forwarder and they learn which services are suitable for particular transport problems.
The S are then confronted with freight enquiries on the telephone, which serve as an example for their own language production. Reading a timetable, the S are to find out about shipment possibilities for a consignment. Moreover, they learn how to deal with calculations, sizes and dimensions.

C: Some standard terms to be found in a freight quotation and the advice of dispatch are taught and practice is given in using them.

D: The section covers the most usual transport documents and the difficulties that may arise from inadequate documents in an L/C transaction. The S are also given practice in transforming a telephone conversation into a German memo.

E: An overview of the 1990 INCOTERMS is given, with special reference to the transfer of cost and risk. The S learn to appreciate these and other factors involved when deciding on a particular INCOTERM.

A
Comparing modes of transport

Methodology

The T could use the pictures of the modes of transport on page 92 (Starter) to elicit the various modes and means of transport that are available to a business. The blackboard or an overhead transparency could be used to draw up an overview.

mode of freight transport	means of freight transport	movement
air	plane (passenger planes with freight compartments, freight only planes)	to fly, to transport by air
land (surface transport)	truck, lorry trailer, road train (Australian), van, pick-up	to truck, to operate, to run, to drive, to transport by road
rail (surface transport)	railway, wagon (covered freight wagon)	to transport by rail
water (surface transport)	ship/vessel, ocean vessel, ro/ro (roll-on-roll-off) vessel, container ship, tanker, liner (Passagierschiff/Linienschiff), ferry, collier (Kohlenschiff), river barge (Last-/Frachtkahn)	to operate, to run, to transport by river or sea

a

Key 🗝 *Key* 🗝 *Key* 🗝 *Key* 🗝

The students compare the various positions listed in the table, thereby exercising their knowledge of comparatives. Make sure that students employ varied expressions in cost comparisons, i.e. is cheaper/dearer than, is less/more expensive than, is higher/lower than, exceeds the cost, undercuts the price, compares favourably with etc.

b

Key 🗝 *Key* 🗝 *Key* 🗝 *Key* 🗝

Costwise, the answer seems to be predetermined: sea is cheaper. However, depending on the preferences of the buyer, cost need not be the decisive factor. Thus, if the machine is very urgently required, the additional expense for air freight will be negligible in the case under consideration and transit time becomes the all important factor.

c

Key 🗝 *Key* 🗝 *Key* 🗝 *Key* 🗝

Although most products can be moved by air, there are certain product types which are more likely than others to be air freighted in an import or export transaction. These include highly fragile products for the electronics industry, which might easily be damaged during the sea voyage, goods needing a lot of surveillance, like precious metal or diamonds that would be considered high-risk for accident or theft-prone land-based or sea transport, and urgent shipments like the supply of medicines or fresh flowers which must be delivered without any delay.

d

Key 🗝 *Key* 🗝 *Key* 🗝 *Key* 🗝

Some suggestions for comparison might be:

	speed	cost	suitable distances	convenience	damage to the environment
road	fairly quick; door-to-door service helps overall speed	running costs still lower than with other forms of transport, but capital cost of vehicles can be very high	local deliveries and medium journeys up to about 500 miles; can be used as a feeder to rail or port/airport	good for easy door-to-door deliveries and short turnaround time	contributes highly to the pollution of the environment
rail	still frequently slower and more unreliable than road, especially since transshipment is necessary for through deliveries	fairly cheap especially for bulk loads/container loads over longer distances	any distance provided time is not that important (or the shipper has the exclusive use of certain trains and a rail siding = Rangiergleis)	relatively poor for traditional break-bulk, better for containerised cargo	good environmental track record with low impact on the environment

e

Methodology

This dialogue should take up the various positions mentioned in the introductory table in a role play. To help students improvise a dialogue like this, let them take notes before starting or do the dialogue after B2 1.

Key 🗝 *Key* 🗝 *Key* 🗝 *Key* 🗝

(Model dialogue)

> Global Fracht, Düsseldorf, Meier. Guten Morgen.

> This is Harry Wong of Suchi Machines. We've got a consignment for Africa for you.

Could I have the consignment details, please?

Yes, of course. It's about a machine which is to be shipped from Hamburg to Transvaal in South Africa. The net weight of the machine is 95 kilograms and the volume of the consignment is 0.6 m³ for ocean cargo and 0.9 m³ for air transport. The ex-works price of the machine is $ 6,000.00.

I see. Let me just make a note of the data. I'll fax you the prices for air and sea transport for comparison this afternoon.

Thank you very much. We'll get in touch with you as soon as we have decided on the most suitable mode of transport for our consignment. Goodbye.

Goodbye and thank you for calling.

B

1 Forwarding agents

a

Key Key Key
1. shipping options
2. country of destination
3. customs clearance
4. livestock
5. to cater for
6. bonded warehousing
7. to customise
8. warehousing
9. cranage
10. heavy haulage

b

Key
1. E.
2. D.
3. J.
4. G.
5. F.
6. I.
7. B.
8. C.
9. H.
10. A.

c

Key Key Key Key
- Transglobe offers transport for all kinds of goods by all means of transport.
- Transports can be LCL and FCL on a scheduled basis.
- All types of project work are dealt with.
- Storage and distribution are undertaken.
- Fairs and Exhibitions are a speciality.
- Transglobe will handle removals and personal effects.

d

Key Key Key Key
1. project services (including e.g. heavy haulage and cranage)
2. warehousing and distribution
3. project services (including e.g. heavy haulage and cranage)
4. LCL air shipments
5. removals and personal effects
6. transport of livestock

e

Key Key Key Key
Transglobe transportiert alle Arten von Gütern mit den unterschiedlichsten Transportträgern als Komplettladung oder als Teilladung mit fahrplanmäßigen Abfahrten. Zudem übernimmt die Firma Transportdienstleistungen bei Großprojekten ebenso wie die Lagerung und Verteilung von Waren. Neben Messe- und Ausstellungsdienstleistungen vervollständigen Umzugsverkehre und die Beförderung von persönlichen Effekten das Leistungsspektrum.

2 Two air freight enquiries

Key Key Key Key

1. Hungarian champagnes for Taiwan

a

1. sheets of thin paper
2. use of packing material made from sheets of heavy paper whose top sheet is grooved and ridged to divide products put into a box
3. not easily damaged if dropped or hit
4. wish good luck
5. initial order to test the quality of a product or service
6. the buildings and land a company uses
7. transferring/loading goods from one means of transport to another
8. money paid for storing goods in a bonded warehouse (to avoid having to pay tax)

9. price for getting goods for a client through the customs
10. value added tax/general sales tax
11. section, part
12. consolidation service, i.e. putting LCL shipments into one container
13. shipment requiring a full container

b and **c**

Key Key Key Key

consignment details:
product: a case of 12 bottles of Hungarian champagne
measurements: 0.4 x 0.4 x 0.23 m
cube: 0.036 cbm
packing: individual bottles wrapped in layers of tissue paper and separated by corrugated paper dividers
weight: 22 kgs
(NB: trial order only; next order for 1m bottles with 100 20-foot containers with a frequency of 2–3 shipments per month)

shipping dates:
presentation of goods at Budapest cargo acceptance: the next day (today not possible)
required time of arrival in Taipei: 11 or 12 June

flight details:
transfer connection (no direct connection)
transshipment via London Heathrow
flight BA 878 Budapest Heathrow, dep. Budapest 09.00, arr. London 11.40
flight BA 26 London Taipei, dep. London 19.25, arr. Taipei 04.25 the next day (all times local times)

price:
cannot be established due to computer failure

d

Dear Caroline,

We've got an urgent shipment of one box with 12 bottles of Hungarian champagne from Budapest to Taipei which is to arrive at its destination on 11th or 12th June.

The box is 0.4 x 0.4 x 0.23 m, approx. 0.036 cbm and has a total weight of 22 kgs. As the bottles are wrapped in layers of tissue paper and separated by corrugated paper dividers they should be quite shockproof and no additional packing will be required on your side.

Please let us know your most favourable all-in rate for individual cargo and, alternatively, for an LCL shipment, should that prove possible under the given conditions. We also need the flight details, i.e. the scheduling and the transit time. The shipment would be delivered to Budapest airport cargo acceptance.

I think you might be interested to know that this is a trial shipment only. If our customer in Taipei likes the champagne, he will very likely place an order for 1m bottles with 100 20-foot containers with a frequency of 2–3 shipments per month!

I look forward to getting your quotation.

Yours,

Horst

e

Methodology

The S should be allowed to (re-)read the tapescript of the telephone air freight enquiry before doing this exercise. They should also be encouraged to do an outline (not a complete written version) of the dialogue, which might include the following points: greeting, small talk, consignment details, shipping dates, flight details and price (c.f. listening comprehension exercise). Also make sure that no partner in the role play delivers a monologue, i.e. students should be reminded to create a true dialogue. More advanced S could make up different details from those mentioned in the instructions. This might even involve different modes of transport.
Sitting back-to-back will help the simulation of a real telephone conversation, if no phones are available.

2. Wellington boots from Frankfurt to Ankara

a

Methodology

To familiarise the S with reading a timetable let them try to explain the details provided for the first flight, which happens to be a direct one, from Frankfurt to Ankara. Then ask them to explain the first transfer connection out of Frankfurt to Ankara. Note that where there is no entry in the validity column, the service will be run during the whole validity period of this particular timetable. The letter codes for airlines and airports are self-explanatory, with TK standing for Turkish Airlines and IST for Istanbul.
As a preparatory exercise you might want to revise how to tell the time with the 24-hour clock and a 12-hour clock. (In transport manuals like this timetable it is customary to use the 24-hour clock.)

Key ⚷ *Key* ⚷ *Key* ⚷ *Key* ⚷

The following flights are possibilities:
- LH 3880 leaving FRA 09.30 am arriving ESB 13.55. This is a direct flight on a B 737.
- A transfer connection which requires a transshipment from flight TK 900 to TK 928 in Istanbul. The flight departs FRA at 18.25 and reaches IST at 22.30 (B 747). The connecting flight bound for ESB departs IST 23.50 and arrives there at 00.50 local time (A 310).

Additional exercise: Enquiring about flights on the phone

Once the students have accomplished these two tasks and found out suitable flights they can act out a telephone conversation between the freight forwarder and Gummifabriken Walter Berndorf.

Verbs expressing movement of planes:

arrivals
to arrive
to land
to reach
to call at

departures
to depart
to start
to take off
to be bound for
to leave

Methodology

Ask the S to bring along a pocket calculator to the classroom, if you intend to do these exercises in class.
As a preliminary exercise you might put some calculations on the blackboard that the students will have to read out in English once they have taken in the info-box on calculations, sizes and dimensions.

b

Key ⚷ *Key* ⚷ *Key* ⚷ *Key* ⚷

The cubic measure of one carton is approx. 0.014 m³.

c

Key ⚷ *Key* ⚷ *Key* ⚷ *Key* ⚷

cubic capacity of container: 5,890 mm x 2,340 mm x 2,400 mm is 33.1 m³; number of units in one container: cubic capacity of one container divided by the cubic measure of one carton is 33.1 m³ divided by 0.014 m³; this equals 2,364 units.

d

Key ⚷ *Key* ⚷ *Key* ⚷ *Key* ⚷

load weight of container: 20,320 kgs (gross) minus 1,800 (tare) equals 18,520 kgs
weight of one carton: 7 kgs (gross)
weight of 2,364 units: 2,364 units times 7 kgs which is 16,548 kgs; this does not exceed the maximum load weight of the container.

e

Key ⚷ *Key* ⚷ *Key* ⚷ *Key* ⚷

Dear Sir or Madam (Dear Sirs),

We have an urgent shipment of fitted kitchens from Gelsenkirchen to Boston, USA, on 24th February.

Please advise us of your most favourable rates for air and sea cargo. Moreover, we would need details on scheduling (departure and arrival times), transit time and frequencies of the services in question as well as the recommended airport/port of departure. Would Düsseldorf be a possibility for air freight or Duisburg for sea cargo?

We look forward to hearing from you soon.

Yours faithfully,

C
Quotation and advice of dispatch

a

Key ⚷ *Key* ⚷ *Key* ⚷ *Key* ⚷

differences

Option 1 FOB (Free on Board) Dalian China	Option 2 CIF (Cost Insurance Freight) Hong Kong
*ocean freight with National Chinese shipping line without a guaranteed service (the ship will wait until it is fully loaded before it sails)	*ocean freight with Transglobe service which is a guaranteed scheduled service
*cost of ocean freight Dalian–Southampton: USD 2,373 per 20ft container (all inclusive and net)	*cost of ocean freight Hong Kong–Southampton USD 1,320 excluding Hong Kong expenses (e.g. handling fees etc.)

similarities

The UK landside charges of PSTG (£) 538.00 _per container_ (i.e. terminal handling, through delivery to Birmingham and Preston) and customs entry and agency and service fee of PSTG 68 per consignment. Errors and omissions are excepted for both offers.

b

Key ⊙⇁ Key ⊙⇁ Key ⊙⇁ Key ⊙⇁

Für die Beförderung von Eichentoilettensitzen von China nach Southampton macht Transglobe folgendes Angebot:
- Wenn der Kunde die Ware FOB Dalian, China, erwirbt, erfolgt der Transport nach Southampton mit der Nationalen Chinesischen Schifffahrtsgesellschaft zu einem Komplettpreis von US$ 2373 pro Container. Allerdings sind die Abfahrtszeiten nicht garantiert.
- Kauft der Kunde die Ware CIF Hongkong, befördert Transglobe die Ware mit einem fahrplanmäßig verkehrenden Schiff nach GB; Auslagen in Hongkong sind in dem angebotenen Preis von US$ 1320 nicht eingeschlossen.
- Die landseitigen Kosten in Großbritannien (Hafenterminalabfertigung, Weitertransport, Zollabfertigung und Speditionsgebühren) sind bei beiden Angeboten gleich.

c

Key ⊙⇁ Key ⊙⇁ Key ⊙⇁ Key ⊙⇁
(Model fax)

TELEFAX

Empfänger / Recipient:
Mr. A. Steptoe
Steptoe & Sons
184 Milton Park
GB Birmingham

Wertholz GmbH
Industriestr. 12
40408 Düsseldorf
Germany
Tel. ++49 (0211) 73 55 11
Fax ++49 (0211) 73 55 21

Telefax No.: ++44 (121) 23 45 66

Datum / Date:
24 March 19..

Bearbeiter / from:
Peter Weiss

Bezug / Subject:
Your consignment of oak toilet seats

Dear Mr Steptoe,

We are pleased to inform you that your consignment of oak toilet seats has been shipped on MS Ever Gentle. It is expected to arrive in Southampton on 2 May. The goods should be unloaded and cleared through customs by 4 May and therefore reach you by 5 May at the latest.
On your advice the individual toilet seats have been packed in strong paper bags with waterproof lining. Polystyrene chips in the six wooden crates containing 20 seats each should provide adequate protection against shock. Your shipping marks and the gross and net weight have been stencilled on the crates.
The documents have been sent to Lloyds Bank, Birmingham and will be handed over to you on acceptance of our B/E.
We hope that the successful execution of your order will lead to repeat orders.

Yours sincerely,

pp _Peter Weiss_

(Export Manager)

d

Key 🗝 Key 🗝 Key 🗝 Key 🗝

Dear Sir or Madam (Dear Sirs),

The consignment of 1000 bottles of STARBRÄU Bier has been shipped on container vessel Norfolk Star in accordance with your instructions today. The Norfolk Star is expected to reach Sydney on 23 August.

The goods have been packed in special crates with reinforced bottoms. Woodshavings will protect the non-returnable bottles against shock.

The crates have been marked JR Boston and have been numbered from 1 – 10. Gross and tare weight as well as caution marks have also been stencilled on.

Please note that the documents will be sent to First National Bank, Boston and handed over after acceptance of our B/E.

We trust that the goods will arrive safely and that we will get repeat orders from you.

Yours faithfully,

e

Dear Mr Brain,

Thank you very much for your order of …

We will dispatch the ordered 10 bales of unbleached natural cotton cloth with the usual markings on BA cargo flight 234 to Birmingham, Air waybill No BA 345678. The day of arrival at your premises in Birmingham will be … on …

The invoice includes the packing material which is non-returnable.

Yours sincerely,

D
Documentation in international trade

Key 🗝 Key 🗝 Key 🗝 Key 🗝

The bank refuses to pay the exporter because there are several inconsistencies between the documents and the terms of the letter of credit.

1. The *certificate of origin* has not been signed by the Chamber of Commerce official.
2. The letter of credit specifies a higher weight than that in the *commercial invoice* (the weight in the L/C is 15,781 kgs, the weight in the commercial invoice 15,718 kgs). Moreover, the marking in the L/C reads DIS Daytona, the marking on the invoice says DS Daytona.
3. The B/L is foul as the container was damaged when presented to the carrier. For L/C transactions a clean B/L is needed.

c

Key 🗝 Key 🗝 Key 🗝 Key 🗝

1. certificate of origin:
* shows where goods have been produced
* can be used to get preferential customs duty rates
* can avoid goods being stopped at import, as without it they might come from a country falling under an import embargo

2. commercial invoice:
* includes all details on the goods, the particulars of payment, shipment, freight and insurance

3. bill of lading:
* proves that the goods have been handed over to the carrier (proof of receipt)
* enables the bearer to collect the goods in the port of destination (proof of ownership; document of title)
* can be used to transfer ownership of the goods (negotiable document of title)
* can be either clean or foul (in apparent good order or not)

d

Key 🗝 Key 🗝 Key 🗝 Key 🗝

Gesprächsnotiz

An: Klaus Wagner
Von: Hans Schumacher
Datum: heute

Gesprächspartner: Terry Venables, Lloyds
Datum des Gesprächs: heute

Betreff: Probleme der Akkreditivabwicklung für Universal Exports aus dem Vertrag mit Daytona Industries

Das Akkreditiv kann aus folgenden Gründen nicht abgewickelt werden:

1. Es wurde versehentlich ein Ursprungszeugnis ohne die nötige Unterschrift des Vertreters der zuständigen Stelle (Vertreter der Handelskammer) vorgelegt. Das unterschriebene Zeugnis habe ich beigelegt.
2. Die Handelsrechnung weist im Vergleich zum Akkreditiv zwei Tippfehler auf. Das Gewicht wurde mit 15 718 kg anstatt mit 15 781 kg ausgewiesen. Zudem wurden die Markierungen auf der Handelsrechnung mit DS Daytona anstatt mit DIS Daytona angegeben. Die Rechnung wurde bereits korrigiert und liegt bei.
3. Das B/L ist nach Aussage von Terry Venables unrein, da der Container bei Übergabe an die

Reederei bereits beschädigt gewesen sei. Bitte den Sachverhalt mit Reederei und Kunden abklären. H.S.

e

Key *Key* *Key* *Key*

1. sea transactions
2. receipt
3. evidence
4. transferable
5. "clean"
6. "foul"
7. non-negotiable
8. airline(s)
9. quantity
10. goods

E
INCOTERMS

b

Key *Key* *Key* *Key*

Frank Muir has a shipment of 10 FCL containers with 1,116 two-piece fashion men's suits each to be shipped from Bremerhaven to Christchurch. He is not sure whether to choose CFR or CPT Christchurch for the transaction and therefore asks Hans Schumacher for advice.

c

Key *Key* *Key* *Key*

similarities	differences
* they are both shipment contracts, i.e. the seller meets his obligations in the country of shipment	* under CFR the risk passes from seller to buyer when the goods have passed the ship's rail
* the seller must pay for the carriage contract, i.e. all the normal transportation cost by the usual route and in the usual manner to the place of destination	* under CPT the risk passes from seller to buyer as soon as they have been handed over to the first carrier
	(So, if the contents of a container are damaged on arrival in the place of destination, under CFR there might be a dispute as to where the damage occurred: If the damage occurred before the container passed the ship's rail, it would be the seller's responsibility; if it occurred afterwards, responsibility would lie with the buyer. Under CPT the risk is with the buyer as soon as the goods are in the hands of the first transport operator.)

d

Methodology

The S should get thoroughly acquainted with the relevant columns in the table on pages 108/109 before attempting to do this exercise and the following ones.

Key *Key* *Key* *Key*

	EXW	DAF	DES	DEQ	DDU	DDP
1. checking, packaging etc.	S	S	S	S	S	S
2. pre-carriage	B	S	S	S	S	S
3. customs formalities (export)	B	S	S	S	S	S
4. loading charges (export)	B	S	S	S	S	S
5. freight charges	B	S	S	S	S	S
6. unloading charges (import)	B	S	B	S	S	S
7. customs clearance (import)	B	B	B	S	B	S
8. on-carriage	B	B	B	B	S	S

e

Key *Key* *Key* *Key*

Seller: CFR or CPT; probably CPT for the reasons pointed out in **c**.
Buyer: DES

f

Methodology

This exercise is only suitable for more advanced groups who have already gained an understanding of Incoterms in their business studies classes.

Key *Key* *Key* *Key*

– Basic bargaining power: Basically the buyer is in a stronger position in such negotiations, especially since he/she has to fund the carriage charges directly or indirectly. This is even more true for goods in a highly competitive market (like the market for medical scanning equipment).
– Availability of discounts for transit arrangements: The seller may have the opportunity of controlling the transit arrangements, when he arranges and funds them. He might, through other contracts, be able to get a discount, through the volume of business generated to a particular trade or route.
– Experience of the trading market/good business relations: Overall the most decisive factors to employ in determining the most acceptable Incoterm are experience of the trading market (which the business partner will trust) and the development of a good

business relationship between seller and buyer on a long-term basis.
- Speed and cost of transport: As there are different ports of discharge involved (Darwin/Melbourne) these factors will also be relevant in the negotiations.

g

Key *Key* *Key* *Key*

1. provide
2. export
3. customs
4. exportation
5. provide
6. destination (discharge is a synonym)
7. obligation
8. destination
9. loss or damage
10. docked
11. destination
12. discharge
13. customs
14. taxes
15. exportation
16. provide
17. transport
18. possession
19. quality
20. packaging

Unit 8

Business and jobs in Europe

Contents/Targets

Unit 8 concentrates on the European Union and on how to apply successfully for a job in Europe. Furthermore, it focuses on international companies and on aspects that should be considered when expanding abroad. It also contains a section on interpreting as a communications skill.

Starter: The starter shows a map of the European Union in 1997 (+ Norway).

A: Reading the Cecchini Report the S discuss the economic advantages (and possible disadvantages) of a single market.

B: The S read an information leaflet on the Wansbeck Business Park and decide whether the business park meets the requirements of a German company that has decided to choose Britain as the seat of its new branch.

C: The S learn about the advantages inherent in large international companies (the multis). They also learn of the equivalents of German companies and ranks in British and American English. A further point covered here is interpreting, which is practised in a role play.

D: Here, the S are given the information necessary for applying for work in Europe, including a list of European countries that young people in Europe find most popular, and some examples of job advertisements and their appropriate applications. This section also contains the names of German school types and their English equivalents. It then goes on to the CV and the student's own application and closes with the interview.

Starter

Methodology

Warm-up: The S name the countries marked on the map.
(Key: Austria, Belgium, Denmark, Finland, France, Germany, Great Britain, Greece, Ireland (or Eire), Italy, Luxemburg, The Netherlands, Norway, Portugal, Spain, Sweden)

Key 🔑 **Key** 🔑 **Key** 🔑 **Key** 🔑

1. All of the marked countries except Norway.
2. This depends on what year this book is used in. In 1995, Austria, Finland and Sweden were the last countries to join the EU.
3. Norway, Poland, Slovakia, The Czech Republic, Switzerland. Possible reasons: Economic problems (new states: Slovakia and The Czech Republic) or the wish to remain neutral and sell to all countries without EU restrictions.

A
The Cecchini report

Methodology

Warm-up: What gave the member countries a motivation to create a European single market? (The T could write the following prompts on the blackboard: benefit, prosperity, frontier restrictions, procurement market, supporting measures, spin-off, price cut, abolition, duty (customs) advantages of scale, incentive)

Key 🔑 **Key** 🔑 **Key** 🔑 **Key** 🔑

1. The reasons are related to what the report predicted:
   – Increase in prosperity of about DM 430 billion
   – New jobs
   – Price cuts for consumers
   – Foreign trade benefits
   – Increase in the EU's ability to compete
2. a) According to the text, yes.
   b) The answer depends on the year. From the viewpoint of 1996, yes.
3. (suggestions)

	Advantages	Disadvantages
Contracts	job mobility in the EU	some countries have low-wage standard contracts
Employment	job mobility and better opportunities to use one's special abilities	more competition at home from foreign countries – this means harder work to survive
Recognition of qualification	greater ease of finding employment abroad	more competition

4. With increasing competition, a company is challenged to find new ways (new marketing strategies, new products, new distribution channels, new markets) in order to survive. In this way growing competition can be an incentive.

B
Expanding abroad

Methodology

Warm-up questions: Does your company have any branches abroad? Do you know any companies with foreign branches? If your company has any branches abroad, have you got a chance to go there for your training? What does the single market mean to your company and its branch?

a

Key 🗝 Key 🗝 Key 🗝 Key 🗝

The industrial park does **not** meet all the requirements. It does not offer a small factory unit and there is no warehouse mentioned.

b

Methodology

Using a large wall map of England, the S try to point Ashington/Newcastle and other places/regions/cities which they think would be attractive as a location for a German subsidiary (different branches). The S should be prepared to explain their suggestions (e.g. excellent transport connections by road and rail, several ports and an airport nearby).

Key 🗝 Key 🗝 Key 🗝 Key 🗝

One important advantage is that the labour costs are lower. Furthermore, Britain still has connections with the former Commonwealth countries, and thus better export chances regarding these markets. As many people in Britain prefer to "buy British", a company putting "Made in England" on its products may have higher sales in England. Last but not least, the transport facilities offered here are very good, too.

C

1 International companies

Key 🗝 Key 🗝 Key 🗝 Key 🗝

1. PLC (England) and Stock Corporation (USA)
2. It means that the liability of the shareholders is limited to that amount of capital that they have invested.
3. If the general partner, who is normally liable for all debts of the partnership, is a limited company, the liability of this firm is reduced to a minimum for all concerned.
4. No. The person only has the job either because his name is so famous that he brings more business to the company, or because he has done something good for the company in the past, and deserves some sort of reward.
5. The powers of the officer with statutory authority are as follows:
   Statutory authority entitles the holder (in the name of his/her company) to carry out all forms of legal and business actions, both in and out of court, that the operation of a commercial business of any type requires. The authority does **not** entitle its holder
   – to sell and mortgage property (unless this permission is separately given),
   – to sign inventories, balances, and tax declarations,
   – to apply (petition) for bankruptcy proceedings to be opened,
   – to dissolve or change the company,
   – to make an oath in the place of the owner of the business,
   – to take on new partners.

2 A meeting in an international company

a

Key 🗝 Key 🗝 Key 🗝 Key 🗝

Holger Manz eröffnet die Sitzung, in der Möglichkeiten diskutiert werden sollen, zwei neuen Konkurrenten auf dem Markt zu begegnen. Eine japanische und eine britische Firma bieten gleichwertige Produkte zu einem um 10 % günstigeren Großhandelspreis an.
Herr Myles-Percival befürwortet eine Modernisierung, die die (Produktions-)Kosten um mindestens 5 % senken könne, jedoch scheint die Finanzierung einer solchen Modernisierung nicht durchführbar zu sein, wie *Miriam Cowie* entgegnet. Ihrer Meinung nach würde das Geld für eine Modernisierung bei der Einführung neuer Produkte fehlen. Zudem sei die Firma durch die derzeitige Rezession ohnehin finanziell belastet, da einige Kunden ihre Aufträge storniert hätten und bei anderen die Zahlungen ausstünden.
Keith Tibbett sieht die Lösung in neuen Produkten und einer neuen Werbestrategie, die im eigenen Hause und nicht von einer Agentur durchgeführt werden sollen, um so die Kunden besser zu erreichen.
Irving Grant sieht die Möglichkeit von Einsparungen durch Großeinkäufe in der Produktion und durch Reduzierung der Sortenvielfalt bei den Rohstoffen.
Holger Manz schließt die kurze Sitzung, die er als durchaus fruchtbar bezeichnet, mit dem Hinweis auf das Sitzungsprotokoll, das am kommenden Tag verteilt werden soll.

b

Key 🗝 *Key* 🗝 *Key* 🗝 *Key* 🗝

1. The companies have started to produce more competitive products (same quality, better price).
2. He proposes to modernise the plant. This will reduce the costs by 5%.
3. He wants to introduce new products and use new advertising – produced inside the firm.
4. Yes, but we don't know who.

3 Interpreting at a meeting

Key
(Role play, Speaker B)

But we've already practically flooded the market with that type of appliance. What's different about this new machine? Why is it a risk for us?

Yes – but our customers have learnt to depend on the quality. We'll keep the regular customers.

Do you mean that we ought to produce a cheap series? I know other companies have done that sort of thing, but I think we're better.

And when the old stock is all sold out? What will happen then?

All right. But don't forget that we have to have money for this. I'll talk to the bank. Let's hope they'll support us.

D
Applying for a job in Europe

Methodology

Warm-up questions: Do you know any people that have done their training outside Germany? If so, where did they train? How did they like it?

a

Key 🗝 *Key* 🗝 *Key* 🗝 *Key* 🗝
(Suggestions)

France and the UK rank at the top of both charts due to their popular languages and life styles. Both countries have attractive capitals and distinctive landscapes and coastlines. Training and studying in England and France used to be a privilege of the upper classes and it is obviously still very attractive for young people in Europe and all around the world.
Germany is probably in the third position for work and training because of high wages and high quality of training, which of course also increases the chances of finding a job in Germany.

Italy and Spain may be popular due to their Mediterranean climate and life style.
The reasons of the unattractiveness of the countries at the bottom of the list may lie in low wages and poor training standards on the one hand and in less attractive cities on the other hand.

b – **e**

Key 🗝 *Key* 🗝 *Key* 🗝 *Key* 🗝

As the S will give different answers and as they will have different priorities, these exercises can be used to start a discussion about branches, jobs and European countries.

1. Studying job advertisements

a

Key 🗝 *Key* 🗝 *Key* 🗝 *Key* 🗝

The answer depends on the Ss' ideas of the ideal job. Advertisement 2 looks most promising as it is an expanding company (good career prospects) and details are given regarding the tasks and requirement and the remuneration. Advertisement 3 looks least promising and least serious since high salaries are promised for a job you learn nothing about.

b

Methodology

Here, Student B has to prepare for all the expected questions using the adverts on page 121 as well as the file. The T should remind the S that they can only choose one company, and not mix the requirements, benefits, etc. More advanced S could try to improvise and include other aspects in their dialogue as well.

Key 🗝 *Key* 🗝 *Key* 🗝 *Key* 🗝
(Suggestions)

1. What date would you expect me to start?
2. Can you tell me about the products/services that you offer/sell?
3. What tasks and responsibilities would I have? Can I have more details about …?
4. I know it's not very important, but what fringe benefits do you offer?
5. What previous experience/qualifications do you require?
6. If I have a knowledge of commerce, will that be of any help?
7. What are the prospects of promotion like?
8. How many hours per week will I normally have to work?

2. Writing a job application

a

Key Key Key Key

1. The German CV requires a photo, the British one does not. (not in text) The German CV usually consists of several pages, whereas the British CV is normally only one page long.
2. Hobbies that could be useful to the prospective employer, such as knowledge of computers, private pilot's licence (PPL), etc.
3. They give the prospective employer his first impression of the applicant. If it is good, the CV will have better chances.
4. This shows that the applicant knows both languages (or is ready to have his CV translated – this means he *really* wants the job).
5. If a person stands out too much, he/she may be the wrong one for the job. On the one hand he/she may have exaggerated in his/her CV in order to stand out, thus losing his/her credibility. On the other hand, a person with extraordinary qualifications may leave the firm again within a short time for another job with better pay and better career prospects.
6. Concentrate on the achievements, successes, and the difference made to the former employer.

b

Key Key Key Key

1. It may not be a must for a business executive to have first-hand experience of working abroad, but it would certainly be an asset when applying for a job.
2. As English is the language of commerce and transport, a person applying for a job abroad will always have an edge over other applicants when speaking English, even if knowledge of English is not required for a particular position.
3. Opinions differ here. The photo is useful if the job is one where the applicant comes into contact with customers frequently. Handwriting is less important. It can only show that the applicant is neat.

c

Methodology

The S copy out the text and insert their own personal data (or invented data, if they wish).

d

Key Key Key Key

1 – D Verlagsangestellte, 2 – C Versicherungsangestellte(r), 3 – B Bankangestellte, 4 – H etwa: Industriekaufmann(-kauffrau)/Angestellte(r) in der Industrie, 5 – K Angestellte(r) in der Werbung, 6 – I EDV-Angestellte(r), 7 – G etwa: Speditionskaufmann(-kauffrau)/Angestellte(r) bei einer Spedition, 8 – A Groß- und Außenhandelskaufleute/Angestellte im Groß- und Außenhandel, 9 – F Angestellte(r) im Hotel- und Gaststättengewerbe, 10 – E Immobilienangestellte

e

Key Key Key Key

bank staff/ savings bank staff	commercial assistant in hotels	clerical staff in wholesale and export	forwarding clerk	advertising clerk	industrial clerk	commercial employee (insurance)
arranging loans	arranging trips	buying from wholesalers	chartering planes	choosing advertising media	cost accounting	covering risks
helping people to save money	chartering planes	buying goods in bulk	negotiating freight prices	informing the public	planning raw-materials purchase	writing polices
		knowing of customs procedures	transporting goods	selling to the public	selling goods abroad	
		planning raw-materials purchase			writing invoices for goods	
		selling goods abroad				
		writing invoices for goods				

f

Key 🗝 Key 🗝 Key 🗝 Key 🗝

Bank staff	helping with export transactions, advising on investments, changing money, arranging mortgages, granting loans
Commercial assistant	taking and making bookings, dealing with complaints, arranging conventions, banquets, etc.
Forwarding clerk	arranging modes of transport, insurance, and packing, booking cargo space, dealing with claims and complaints
Advertising clerk	dealing with accounts, arranging appointments with sponsors, placing advertisements in the media, arranging advertising shows, fairs, exhibitions and demonstrations
Industrial clerk	doing the inventory, buying goods for resale, coordinating commercial and industrial aspects
Commercial employee (insurance)	contacting new customers, investigating claims, re-insuring large policies, conducting correspondence, public relations work, filling in forms
Data processing clerk	programming computers, writing programmes, EDP-work, troubleshooting (retrieving lost programmes and texts), doing layout work
Estate agency staff	inspecting premises and estates fur buying and selling, doing correspondence, making offers, negotiating terms of rent or payment, administrating houses for absent owners, making arrangements for tenants, repairs, etc.

3. The interview

a

Methodology

The T writes the list on the blackboard using suggestions from the S. The T may have to complete the list.

b

Methodology

Several groups of S or the whole class should do this task.

c

Methodology

The T should remind the S that not only inappropriate questions and answers should be avoided. Look at the picture. How would you react to such a candidate? What is he doing wrong? Would you wear such clothes in an interview?

d

Key 🗝 Key 🗝 Key 🗝 Key 🗝
(Model role play)

Good morning, Mr/Miss/Ms ...

Good morning.

Did you find us all right?

Oh, yes. It was in fact quite easy to get here.

Would you like a coffee?

Yes, please, I'd love one.

Now, what made you apply for the position?

Well, I saw your advertisement in the ... (name of the newspaper). I've always been interested in the tourism/chemical/car/computer/pharmaceutical ... industry and I feel that I meet the requirements for the job perfectly.

Could you tell me something about your educational and professional background?

I went to a vocational school from 19... until 19... and got my first job as an "Industriekaufmann" in 19...

56 · Unit 8

Oh yes, I see. What subjects did you learn at school?

"Industriekaufmann" is roughly the same as an assistant in an industrial business.

The curriculum comprised – among other subjects – business administration, accounting, storekeeping, purchasing, distribution, sales and marketing.

Well, have you ever worked in an advertising department?

No, but I worked in the marketing department at … where I was in charge of placing advertisements in newspapers and special interest magazines.

Very good. Do you happen to know anything about our company?

Yes, your secretary kindly sent me some information along with the invitation to the interview.

So you have probably read that we do business around the world?

Yes, I have. Will there be any travelling involved in the position advertised?

Not in the first year. But we expect our employees to take part in fairs and exhibitions in order to better keep in touch with the competition.

That sounds very interesting.

As we've been doing more and more business with South America in the past few years, Spanish has become important for us.
Do you speak Spanish by any chance?

I'm afraid my command of Spanish is not very good, but I'm willing to learn and improve it if necessary.

Now, have you got any questions?

Yes. Could you give me some information about the tasks involved in the job, the working hours and – last but not least – about the starting salary?

Yes, of course. We expect the successful applicant to coordinate our advertising campaigns with our business partners in South America. You would – however – be made familiar with this task in the first year, assisting Ms Shallis who is leaving us next year. As to working hours, we have flexitime, so you start between 7 am and 9 am, and you finish work between 4 pm and 6 pm. You would start with a salary of £ 15,500 rising to £ 18,000 after the probationary period. After that, the salary would be reviewed annually.

That's all quite attractive and I really hope my application will be considered.

Well, we'll let you know about our decision in about two

weeks. Thank you for coming.

Thank you for the invitation. Goodbye.

E
The "Brain Drain"

Key 🔑 *Key* 🔑 *Key* 🔑 *Key* 🔑

Die Überschrift bezieht sich auf jene Leute, die ins Ausland gehen, um dort mehr Geld zu verdienen oder interessantere Arbeit zu bekommen. Auf diese Weise geht den Heimatländern dieser Experten viel Wissen verloren.

Nach Aussage von Personalberatern sind die Berufsaussichten in Europa und Übersee für in Großbritannien ausgebildete Spezialisten der Informationstechnologie in diesem Jahr besser denn je. Wer das große Geld sucht, ist in Europa am besten aufgehoben. Wer einen anderen Lebensstil sucht, in Amerika.

Obwohl das Anfangsgehalt in Amerika normalerweise niedriger sei als in Großbritannien, gäbe es andere Vorteile, so Herr Coverman, ein leitender Angestellter bei einer Personalberatung. So könne man z. B. entweder seine Kenntnisse erweitern oder durch seine mehrjährige Erfahrung in Amerika seine beruflichen Chancen in Europa verbessern.

Gehaltssteigerungen von einem Vielfachen des Anfangsgehalts bis hin zu $350 000 im Jahr seien nach Aussage einer nicht näher genannten Person in Amerika möglich.

Die Gehälter auf dem europäischen Festland seien gewöhnlich höher als die in Großbritannien. So könne ein Programmierer nach Aussage von Personalberatern auf dem Festland ca. 50 % mehr verdienen. Allerdings sei die Einstellung gegenüber den britischen Informatikern in Europa nicht immer so positiv wie in Amerika. Zum einen würden die Briten oft als unbeständig und labil angesehen, und zum anderen stelle die Sprachbarriere in vielen europäischen Ländern ein großes Problem dar. Wer die entsprechende Sprache beherrsche, meint in diesem Zusammenhang Herr Harris, ein Direktor der OCC-Berater, der könne in Spanien oder in Deutschland viel Geld verdienen.

Photocopiable grammar exercises

Comparison of Adjectives
(Grammar survey, page 131)

a
Put in adjectives in the correct form (positive, comparative, or superlative). Use "the" and "than" if necessary.

H. A. T. Remscheid is one of _____ (1. old) companies in the district. There are many that are _____ (2. famous), but none that can compare with it. They have been working on press plates for _____ (3. much) 120 years, and now, they have started a _____ (4. new) line: tools for making multilayer circuit boards (Multilayer-Platinen). That's _____ (5. late) thing on the market, you know.

b
Rewrite the following sentences to give the same contents, but using the adjective(s) in brackets in the comparative and superlative forms.

1. The letter of credit is a complex method of payment and the bill of exchange is simple (understandable).

2. In the States, payment in cash is regarded as not very honest compared to payment by credit card (honest).

3. In my opinion, nothing can surpass the new "Arkona" car (good).

4. There is not as much money in his account as in the company's (little).

5. Everything in the world is better than that company's reputation (bad).

Tenses
(Grammar survey, page 131-134)

a
Put in either the simple present or the present continuous.

As you can see, John, we _____ (1. not, have) a lot of free time in this department. There is always a lot of work, and even now, at 4 p.m., the orders usually _____ (2. arrive). Diana, over there in the corner, _____ (3. work) on an order she received this morning. She _____ (4. always complain) about working overtime, although she _____ (5. get) time off for it. We can't disturb her now. She _____ (6. want) to finish her correspondence quickly, because she _____ (7. meet) her sister at the airport at 6 p.m. Her sister _____ (8. study) art in New York, but she _____ (9. visit) Diana every year. Oh, excuse me John, but my telephone _____ (10. ring).

b
Simple past or present perfect?

We _____ (1. launch) our new product line last year. The sales of this line _____ (2. be) quite promising so far. Unfortunately, two new competitors _____ (3. appear) on the market only 4 weeks ago. We _____ (4. know) these two companies for 3 years now. Competition from abroad _____ (5. take) away quite a lot of our business. This trend _____ (6. start) two years ago, and it is still continuing. Up to now, we _____ (7. not, suffer) too much. On the other hand, many of our business associates _____ (8. must) branch out into other lines as they simply _____ (9. not, be) competitive enough. To help them, we _____ (10. enter) into a dual-franchise deal where we sell their goods and they sell ours.

c
Past simple, past continuous, present perfect simple or continuous?

The Bad News and the Good

The following is an interview between Ron Scott, a business reporter, and Terry McConnell, the junior manager of the Ellington Machine Company.

RS: How _____ (1. your company/do) in the last six months, since you _____ (2. start) the modernisation?
TM: So far, we _____ (3. only /manage) to get part of the company modernised; it _____ (4. be) easy to take the first steps, but now, we have to work out everything we do very carefully.
RS: What do you mean by that? _____ (5. Be/not) the first steps just as hard to decide on as the later ones?
TM: By no means. When we _____ (6. decide) to do the modernising, we just _____ (7. start) by buying some new machines already set up for CNC control.
RS: Well, what's wrong with that? Why _____ (8. you/not/manage) to get more done in the meantime?
TM: We _____ (9. find) out that the increased efficiency _____ (10. not/match) the rest of the works. While we _____ (11. try) to produce as much as possible in the centre of the production process, the first and last parts _____ (12. lag) behind. This meant that we sometimes _____ (13. have) to wait for semi-finished parts to put into the CNC process, and to stockpile them until they _____ (14. be) needed. Because of this, we _____ (15. have) to reorganise the whole process, including the floor plan: We _____ (16. have) to arrange for temporary placing of the new machines in the production process, so that they _____ (17. can) be moved to suit the rest of the machines later. We _____ (18. work) on this for two months now.
RS: I see that you _____ (19. find) out some of the problems in modernisation.
TM: Yes, but I _____ (20. only/tell) you one side of the affair. We _____ _____ (21. be able) to increase production by 20%, and we _____ _____ (22. already/negotiate) two new contracts, one of them with the Government.
RS: I see. By the way, how long _____ (23. you/work) in the company?
TM: Oh, I …

Annotations:
lag – to go slower than the rest / stockpile – to store for future use / floor plan – arrangement of the machines with relation to one another

"Going to" or "will"?
(Grammar survey, page133/34)

a
Put in the future with "going to" or "will". Be ready to justify your choice.

1. Goodbye. We _____ (see) you next Friday.
2. What _____ (the secretary/do) in your absence?
3. I _____ (not/visit) any museums when I'm in Amsterdam.
4. I hear that Hermann KG _____ (adopt) new products into their range.
5. Have you heard that the factory is closing down? – Yes, I suppose we _____ (lose) a lot of customers.
6. Look at those figures. We _____ (lose) market shares.
7. What _____ (you/do) if LSG Corporation can't supply the milling machine on time?
8. Hold the line, please, I _____ (put) you through.

b
Use the correct future forms (going to/will/ing-form) in the following text.

„Well, if you want to know about my plans on my next holidays, I can tell you this. I _____ (1. travel) through North Rhine-Westphalia. I think I _____ (2.travel) along the Rhine. The people at the travel agency told me that I _____ (3. have) plenty of time every day for seeing the sights. I _____ (4. not/just/relax) there. I _____ (5. probably/look) for business opportunities. The business press expects that the Rhine-Ruhr region _____ (6. experience) a boom within the next ten years. On 1 July, at the end of my holidays, I _____ (7. meet) an old friend of mine in Cologne.

Reported Speech
(Grammar survey, page 134)

Reporting Statements / Replies
He / The representative, etc.
remarked/pointed out/stated/declared/mentioned/maintained/added/explained/told the meeting/informed the meeting/insisted/answered

Reporting Suggestions / Advice
"We could run this ad nationally."
He suggested/proposed/advised/recommended running the ad nationally.

Reporting Requests
Requesting Action
"Do you think you could give him the message?"
The client wanted /asked / requested the agency to give him the message.

Requesting Information
"Does market research have any data about the market situation in Germany?" "Where will the next meeting take place?" The Sales Director asked / inquired / wanted to know / whether (if) market research had any data on the market situation in Germany. … where the meeting would take place.

Reporting Agreement and Refusal of Actions
"We will/won't try to get a second opinion." The representatives agreed to / refused to obtain a second opinion.

Reporting Opinions
"I believe we will lose our market leader position if we do not adapt to the market." He / She believed / considered / thought / was of the opinion that they would lose their market leader position if they did not adapt to the market.

Reporting Agreement and Disagreement with Opinion

The participants agreed (that … / with …)
                accepted that …
                were in favour of …
                were in full agreement (about … / with …)
The participants did not agree (that … / with …)
                disagreed (with …)
                did not accept that …
                found it unacceptable …

Reporting Expectations / Wishes
"You should finish the report by next week." (The client) wanted / expected / wished the agency to finish the report by the following week.

Reporting Offers / Promises / Threats
"I'll change the media schedule again." He / She offered / promised / threatened to change the media schedule again.

Change into indirect speech using an appropriate introductory expression from the above list.

1. Mr White on the phone to Mr Green's secretary: "I'd like to meet Mr Green tomorrow."
   _____

2. Secretary addressing back to Mr Green: "I won't work overtime."
   _____

3. Purchsing manager to inefficient supplier: "We will look for another supplier if the consignment is delayed again."
   _____

4. Trainee to shop assistant: "What was the price for our music software last year?"
   _____

5. Managing director: "Couldn't we intensify our sales promotion measures?"
   _____

6. Salesman to secretary: "Was the meeting here or in the head office?"
   _____

7. Proprietor of a shop after a traveller's visit: "I think we'll be able to sell quite a few of the new products."
   _____

8. Computer salesperson to customer: "If you want, we can offer you a service contract for your new equipment."

9. Engineer to publicity department: "We have developed a new type of transistor."

10. Translation agency to client: "We're sorry, but our translators won't work over the weekend."

Conditionals
(Grammar survey, page 135)

a
Fill in the correct verb form either in the if clause or the main clause.

1. If the damage had not been so obvious, the Danish hotel _____ (install) the brass switches.
2. The Purchasing Manager will accept the delivery if the goods _____ (pass) the check in the receiving department.
3. If the supplier _____ (send) the products in time, the order would be executed properly.
4. If we _____ (know) that McMillan's offer was more competitive than Hanson's, we would have given them the order.
5. Certainly our firm _____ (not, do) business with Ferguson's if all their goods are as bad as their samples.
6. We _____ (exchange) the defective goods for faultless ones if you returned the consignment immediately.
7. If the customer had not found out that something was wrong with the goods, he _____ _____ (not, write) a complaint.
8. If you _____ (be prepared) to keep the slightly damaged products, we would invoice them at 40 % of the list price.

b
Translate the following sentences into English.

1. Wäre die Ware nicht ungenügend verpackt gewesen, hätte der Schaden vermieden werden können.

2. Wenn Sie die bestellten Glühbirnen nicht bis zum 10. Juni liefern, werden wir von Ihnen Entschädigung verlangen.

3. Wir würden jedoch die Artikel behalten, wenn Sie uns einen Preisnachlass von 25 % gewährten.

4. Günter Möbius hätte den Brief nicht geschrieben, wenn die Handtuchhalter rechtzeitig und in der richtigen Ausführung zugesandt worden wären.

5. Wenn Sie Ihre Zahlungsbedingungen änderten, würden wir Ihr Angebot annehmen.

6. Wenn Sie Ihre Qualitätssicherung nicht verbessern, werden wir uns einen neuen Lieferanten suchen.

7. Die Lieferung wäre bei Ihnen rechtzeitig angekommen, wenn es nicht einen Streik in unserer Fabrik in Birmingham gegeben hätte.

8. Wenn unsere Kunden von dem neuen Produkt begeistert sind, wird die Nachfrage danach stark ansteigen.

9. Sie sollten uns eine Erklärung des Problems geben, wenn Sie der Meinung sind, Sie müssten die gelieferte Ware ablehnen.

10. Wir hätten Ihnen die noch fehlenden zwanzig Teile umgehend zugesandt, wenn wir vom Konkurs unseres Hauptlieferanten früher erfahren hätten.

Passive Voice
(Grammar survey, page 136)

a
Change these sentences into the passive voice.

1. Schmidt & Co. have transferred Paul Meyer to H&F in Birmingham.

2. The company cannot produce all parts itself.

3. The purchasing department compares incoming quotations.

4. The supplier will guarantee a constant high-quality product.

5. The company has also requested construction drawings and samples.

6. More and more companies consider environmental factors when planning new products.

7. They checked the products regarding their ecological qualities.

8. They say the company is insolvent.

9. The personnel manager is interviewing two applicants.

10. The advising bank will send the documents to the issuing bank.

b
Put the verbs in brackets into the correct passive voice.

1. One copy _____ (place) on the parts and the other one _____ (pass) on to another department. (simple present)
2. Computers _____ (recently introduce) into a lot of companies. (Present perfect)
3. If a new supplier _____ (accept), he/she _____ (visit) by representatives of the enquiring firm. (Simple present/will-future)
4. Quotations _____ (must compare) considering various factors. (Simple present)
5. Numerous new parts _____ (need) before we can produce this new article. (Future)
6. Last year's prices _____ (regard) as too low to cover the costs. (Simple past)
7. She informed the employees that almost 50% of the workers _____ (make) redundant. (Past perfect)
8. Examinations in English for Technicians _____ (hold) from next February on by the Chamber of Commerce and Industry. (Future)
9. How _____ the error _____ (can, overlook)? (Present perfect)
10. New arrivals _____ (must, register) at the central office. (Simple past)

c
Translate the following sentences.

1. In zwei Wochen werden 2000 Federn (springs) benötigt.

2. Die Exportabteilung wurde letzte Woche über unseren Besuch informiert.

3. Es wir erwartet, dass die Bestellung pünktlich geliefert wird.

4. Jeder neue Lieferant wird geprüft.

5. Umweltfreundliche Produkte sollen bevorzugt werden.

6. Die Lieferung kann nicht angenommen werden, da sich die Waren als fehlerhaft herausstellten.

7. Unsere Zahlungsbedingungen müssen neu ausgehandelt werden.
   _____

8. Bevor die Waren gelagert wurden, waren sie sorgfältig geprüft worden.
   _____

Infinitive
(Grammar survey, page 136)

a
Use a suitable auxiliary verb and infinitive (with or without "to"), so that the following sentences make sense. Some hints are given in brackets.

1. The customer _____ the letter of credit before the supplier starts production. (eröffnen)
2. You _____ that letter if you don't want to. (beantworten)
3. He has the chance; he _____ the items at a bargain price, but he doesn't want to. (einkaufen)
4. The regulations tell us what we _____, but not what we _____. (tun sollen, nicht dürfen)

b
Translate the following sentences into English, using an infinitive preceded by "to".

1. Ihm wird verboten werden, die Korrespondenz zu lesen.
   _____

2. Es ist schwer zu begreifen, weshalb wir einen Verlust hatten.
   _____

3. Er weiß nicht, wie er den Kunden erreichen kann.
   _____

4. Die Anzeige war zwar amüsant zu lesen, jedoch für unsere Zwecke völlig uninteressant.
   _____

5. Die deutsche Industrie wird sehr darauf erpicht sein, die neuen Techniken zu lernen.
   _____

Gerund
(Grammar survey, page 136)

Using a suitable verb (in the "-ing form" where necessary) list, complete the following sentences.

avoid	hate	fire	buy
meet	hand	get	talk
try	sell	shop	

1. Since we could not get in touch with the repairman, John suggested _____ to make the repair himself.
2. Do you mind _____ me the report?
3. Some customers _____ paying their invoices.

4. We look foward to _____ you next week.
5. The company retrains people instead of _____ them.
6. Do you remember _____ to Mr Winter?
7. The survey shows that most customers prefer _____ in department stores.
8. _____ and _____ is our business.
9. We usually _____ sending reminders, but this time there is no other way.
10. The client is interested in _____ information on our new product range.

Participle
(Grammar survey, page 137)

a
Use the correct participial form (e.g. selling, sold) as an adjective in the following sentences:

1. The _____ (emerge) trend will be clearly seen in a couple of months.
2. Before _____ (start) our advertising campaign, we have to define the target group.
3. The _____ (finish) product will be packed for transport; its _____ (intend) destination is then marked on the packing.
4. The _____ (finish) process is most important as the appearance of the product makes it sell.
5. I would like to speak to the _____ (manage) director to find out some details.
6. The consignment _____ (arrive) this morning was damaged.
7. The _____ (issue) L/C is a guarantee to the seller.
8. The _____ (issue) bank informed the German bank.

b
Use a participial form to replace the relative clauses in italics.

1. The services *that cater* for your needs are expensive.
   _____

2. I was happy to get rid of the goods *that were gathering* dust in the store.
   _____

3. The letters *which were written* last year have been filed; the clerk *who filed* them is now employed for other duties.
   _____

4. The mode of transport *that was selected* was not the cheapest because the person *who made* the selection did not know all the facts.
   _____

5. The services *that are based* on the use of computers have become very popular.
   _____

6. The department *that has been chosen* is Marketing.
   _____

7. The persons *who have effected* the changes have been praised.
   _____

8. The contract *that is enclosed* is only a draft.
   _____

Key

Comparison of Adjectives

a
1. the oldest
2. more famous
3. more than
4. new
5. the latest

b
1. The bill of exchange is more understandable than the letter of credit.
2. In the States, payment by credit card is regarded as more honest than payment by cash.
3. In my opinion, the new "Arkona" car is the best.
4. There is less money in his account than in the company's.
5. That company's reputation is the worst in the world.

Note: Other variants of these sentences are easily possible.

Tenses

a
1. don't have
2. arrive
3. is working
4. is always complaining
5. gets
6. wants
7. is meeting
8. is studying
9. visits
10. is ringing

b
1. launched
2. have been
3. appeared
4. have known
5. has taken
6. started
7. have not suffered
8. have had to
9. were not
10. have entered

c
1. has your company been doing
2. started
3. have only managed
4. was
5. Weren't
6. decided
7. started
8. haven't you managed
9. found
10. didn't match
11. were trying
12. were lagging
13. had
14. were
15. have had
16. had
17. could
18. have been working
19. 've found
20. 've only told
21. 've been able
22. 've already negotiated
23. have you been working

"Going to" or "will"?

a
1. will see
2. is your secretary going to do
3. 'm not going to visit
4. is going to adopt
5. will lose
6. are going to lose
7. are you going to do
8. 'll put

b
1. 'm going to travel (intention – the speaker is describing his plans)
2. will travel (simple prediction following "think")
3. 'm going to have (inevitable future – the travel agency intends the speaker to have time)
4. 'm not just going to relax (intention)
5. will probably look (simple prediction following an intention)
6. will experience (prediction – made by the experts of the business press)
7. 'm meeting (firmly-planned future including a stated time)

Reported Speech

1. Mr White asked to meet Mr Green the next / following day.
2. The secretary refused to work overtime.
3. The purchasing manager threatened (the inefficient supplier) to look for another supplier if the consignment was delayed again.
4. The trainee asked the shop assistant what the price for their music software had been the year before.
5. The managing director suggested / proposed intensifying their promotion measures.
6. The salesman asked the secretary whether the meeting had been there or in the head office.
7. The proprietor of the shop believed/was of the opinion that/thought they would be able to sell quite a few of the new products.

8. The computer salesperson offered the customer a service contract for his/her new equipment.
9. The engineer informed/told the publicity department (let the publicity department know) that they had developed a new type of transistor.
10. The translation agency regretfully informed the client that its translators wouldn't work over the weekend.

Conditionals

a
1. would have installed
2. pass
3. sent
4. had known
5. will not do
6. would exchange
7. would not have written
8. were prepared

b
1. If the goods had not been packed inadequately, the damage would have been avoided.
2. If you do not deliver the ordered bulbs by 10th June, we will claim compensation from you.
3. However, we would keep the articles if you granted us a discount of 25%.
4. Günter Möbius would not have written the letter if the towel holders had been sent on time and in the correct quality.
5. If you changed your terms of payment, we would accept your offer.
6. If you do not improve your quality assurance, we will look for a new supplier.
7. The consignment would have arrived on time if there had not been a strike in our factory in Birmingham.
8. If our customers are enthusiastic about the new product, the demand for it will rise rapidly.
9. You should give us an explanation of the problem if you think you have to refuse the proper consignment.
10. We would have sent you the twenty missing parts immediately if we had heard about the bankruptcy of our main supplier earlier.

Passive Voice

a
1. Paul Meyer has been transferred to H&F in Birmingham by Schmidt & Co.
2. All parts cannot be produced by the company itself.
3. Incoming quotations are compared by the purchasing department.
4. A constant high-quality product will be guaranteed by the supplier.
5. Construction drawings and samples have also been requested by the company.
6. Environmental factors are considered by more and more companies when planning new products.
7. The products were checked regarding their ecological qualities.
8. The company is said to be insolvent.
9. Two applicants are being interviewed by the personnel manager.
10. The documents will be sent to the issuing bank by the advising bank.

b
1. is placed, is passed
2. have recently been introduced
3. is accepted, will be visited
4. must be compared
5. will be needed
6. were regarded
7. had been made
8. will be held
9. can the error have been overlooked?
10. had to be registered

c
1. 2,000 springs will be needed (required) in two weeks.
2. The export department was informed about our visit last week.
3. It is expected that the order will be shipped (sent off, delivered) on time.
4. Every new supplier is checked.
5. Environmentally-friendly products must/are to be given preference.
6. The delivery (shipment, consignment) cannot be accepted since the goods were (have been) found to be faulty.
7. Our terms (conditions) of payment must be renegotiated.
8. Before the goods were stored they had been carefully checked.

Infinitive

a
1. must open
2. needn't answer (don't need to answer)
3. can buy
4. should do (ought to do), must not do

b
1. He will be forbidden to read the correspondence.
2. It's hard to understand why we had a loss.

3. He doesn't know how to get in touch with (to reach) the customer.
4. The advertisement was amusing to read but completely uninteresting for our purposes. (Although the advert was amusing to read, it was completely uninteresting for our purposes.)
5. The German industry will be very eager to learn the new techniques.

Gerund

1. trying
2. handing
3. hate/avoid
4. meeting
5. firing
6. talking
7. shopping
8. Buying (and) selling
9. avoid/hate
10. getting

Participle

a
1. emerging
2. starting
3. finished, intended
4. finishing
5. managing
6. arriving
7. issued
8. issuing

b
1. catering
2. gathering
3. written, filing
4. selected, making
5. based
6. chosen
7. effecting
8. enclosed

Commercial Correspondence (Prüfungsaufgaben)

Key

1. Enquiry

(Note: Several variants are given for some of the expressions. Please remember that the following letters are real business letters; they are not translations except in the sense that all the details are present. The S should also be reminded that the letters in the Student's Book are "skeleton" letters; they should be "fleshed out" to make them into real ones.)

H.A.T.
Herbert Anton Thomas GmbH
Ibachtal 9   42859 Remscheid
Tel.: 02191/667430   Fax: 02191/667448

Arthur & Ball
152 Holloway Road
London N7 8LX
Great Britain

4 March, ...

Dear Sir or Madam,

We are a medium-sized manufacturer of press tools in Germany, and we continually need machines that guarantee the highest-possible/best-possible surface quality.

Our mutual business friend, D. I. Moon Ltd., Penzance, has informed us that you have launched a line of completely new polishing machines. We would appreciate it if you could send us detailed literature/sales material/brochures on these machines together with the appropriate price lists.

Since/As we might be placing considerable orders, please let us know your most favourable terms of delivery and payment as well as your best prices. If your quotation appears acceptable, we shall place a trial order.

We look forward to an early reply./We look forward to hearing from you soon.

Yours faithfully,
(signature)

Hanna Ott   *(the S should either sign with their own name or invent a name)*

Purchasing Manager
H.A.T. GmbH

2. Quotation

Arthur & Ball

Polishing Machines
152 Holloway Road
London N7 8LX
England

H.A.T.
Herbert Anton Thomas GmbH
Purchasing Department
Att.: Ms Ott
Ibachtal 9
42859 Remscheid

5 March, …

Dear Ms Ott,

Your enquiry of 4 March, …

Thank you very much/We should like to thank you for your enquiry, which we received this morning.

As requested, we are sending you our general catalogue and 2 special leaflets by the same mail/under separate cover. The price lists and our terms of payment and delivery are enclosed as well.*

We should be pleased to enter into business relations with your company, since we have had no business contacts with Germany so far. If we can agree on suitable conditions, we might be able to offer you the sole agency for our machines in Germany.

Should you be interested in this offer, our general manager, Erik Ball, would be prepared to visit your company in Remscheid and discuss all further details.

We would appreciate an early reply.

Yours sincerely,

(signature)

Peter Jenkins   *(the S should invent a name and any other details)*
Sales Manager
Arthur & Ball
Polishing Machines

---

* *Note: Some S might ask why no "Encl." appears at the end of this letter. This is because the price lists, etc. are enclosed with the separate letter that is being sent off.*

3. Order

H.A.T.
Herbert Anton Thomas GmbH
Ibachtal 9   42859 Remscheid
Tel.: 02191/667430   Fax: 02191/667448

Arthur & Ball
152 Holloway Road
Att.: Peter Jenkins
London N7 8LX
England

8 March, …

Dear Mr Jenkins,

Trial Order

We wish to thank you for your quotation, which we have read with interest. Based on this, we would be interested in placing a trial order for:

   1 Polishing Machine, No. 235/7 ((Model/Type) A).

However, the time of delivery (7 weeks) appears to be too long. We would appreciate delivery in 5 weeks. Is that possible? If the machine comes up to our expectations/meets our requirements fully, we should be prepared to place an order for 80 machines*.

As to/With regard to/Concerning the question of the sole agency, we should like to receive more details. Could this be extended, if necessary, to Poland and the CIS? What assistance would you be able to offer us?

We look forward to your early reply.

Yours sincerely,

(signature)

Hanna Ott
Purchasing Manager
H.A.T. GmbH

---

* Note: It might be useful at this point (if not beforehand) to inform the S that in correct English, "Stück" = "Stückzahl" only means pieces if these are actually (broken-off or cut-off) parts of a larger thing. Thus we can say "pieces of metal", "pieces of cloth", but not pieces of machines. When a machine is in pieces, it is unusable!

4. Acknowledgement of Order

Arthur & Ball

Polishing Machines
152 Holloway Road
London N7 8LX
England

H.A.T. GmbH
Att.: Ms Ott
Ibachtal 9
42859 Remscheid
Germany

11 March, …

Dear Ms Ott,

Acknowledgement of Order

Thank you very much for your trial order, No. G/1/235 for the polishing machine No. 235/7 (Model A), which we have received today.

We are sending you enclosed/in the enclosure our acknowledgement form No. 1057, from which you may learn/see that the machine can be sent off at a price of £14,665.76 CIF Antwerp (including packing) and with a time of delivery reduced to 6 weeks (instead of 7).

If you order 100 units, we should be pleased to grant/allow you a quantity discount/discount of 10%.

Payment should be made/effected by transfer of the invoice amount to our account No. 26338/C at/with … Bank, London.

Loading will take place at Tilbury Docks on … .

We assure you that we shall execute further orders promptly and carefully, and we should be pleased to receive your further correspondence.

Yours sincerely,

(Unterschrift)

Peter Jenkins
Sales Manager
Arthur & Ball
Polishing Machines

Encl.: Acknowledgement form No. 1057.

5. Complaint

H.A.T.
Herbert Anton Thomas GmbH
Ibachtal 9   42859 Remscheid
Tel.: 02191/667430   Fax: 02191/667448

Messrs. Arthur & Ball
152 Holloway Road
London N7 8LX
England

5 November, ...

Dear Mr Jenkins,

Your shipment of 5 November, ...

We have been purchasing/buying polishing machines from your company for two years, and up to now there has never been a cause for complaint.

We regret to inform you, however, that the latest shipment of spare parts was not satisfactory for the following reasons/due to the following:

1. Case 1.   (2 drive motors)
   These appear to have been damaged/It appears that these were damaged during shipment. Water has entered the case and destroyed 2 printed-wiring boards.
2. Case 4.   Instead of polishing heads the case contained 2 drive motors.
3. Case 5.   This case was missing/not delivered.

As we are unable to repair the damaged machines (and as the additional drive motors in case 4 are not the model required), we will have delays in our production.

We would really appreciate it if you could inform us immediately about what you intend to do about this. Could you send us a fax within 24 hours, giving details of how you wish to regulate this matter?

As time is pressing we will be forced to look elsewhere for another supplier if no swift settlement can be reached.

Yours sincerely,

(Signature)

Hanna Ott
Purchasing Department
H.A.T. GmbH

6. Reminder

Arthur & Ball

Polishing Machines
152 Holloway Road
London N7 8LX
England

H.A.T. GmbH
Ibachtal 9
42859 Remscheid
Germany

6 July, …

Dear Mr/Ms …

Outstanding payments

On checking your account, we have noticed that the payments for our last two consignments/shipments to you have not yet been settled:

Order No. FU 2/12/12/8 of 12 December, …, for 16 machines No. I/1/2/2P, sent off on 8 February, …, and

Order No. FU 3/19/01/9 of 19 January, …, for 18 machines No. 124C/41, sent off on 14 March, …

We assume that this can only be due to an oversight, but would ask you to check our account number in your records, since we had a computer reorganisation 6 months ago.

As we also have to pay our own suppliers, we would ask for a transfer of the outstanding amount/amount due to our account No. 26338/C at/with … Bank, London as soon as possible.

We are sure/certain that you will do everything possible to maintain our business relations, which have been very good up to now.

Yours sincerely

(Signature)

Accounts Manager
Arthur & Ball
Polishing Machines

... Bank

STANDING ORDER MANDATE

To: ... Bank Plc	Address:
Please debit my account	Account No.
	Account Name
and pay	Bank: / Branch Title (not address):
	Sort Code
	Account No.
	Beneficiary
Quoting reference	[reference box] — This instruction cancels any previous order in favour of the beneficiary named above, under this reference
at the following intervals	Day/date: / Weekly, monthly, annually, other:
the sum of	Regular amount: £ —
	Amount in words:
commencing	Date and amount of first payment: Now* or / / £ —	until	Date and amount of last payment: Until you receive further notice from me/us in writing* or / / £ —

*delete if not applicable

Special Instructions	
Signature(s)	Date / /

Note: The Bank will not undertake to: (i) make any reference to Value Added Tax or other indeterminate element. (ii) advise payer's address to beneficiary. (iii) advise beneficiary of inability to pay. (iv) request beneficiary's banker to advise beneficiary or receipt or payment.

PHOTOCOPIABLE FORMS · 77

..........., the .... 19..... For ....

Bill of Exchange (............ unpaid)

At .... pay against this .... sight bills on .... as advised by

to the order of ....

payable in legal currency at the collecting banks drawing rate for .... which place to Account

value ....

To ....

No.

LETTRE DE VOITURE INTERNATIONALE CMR INTERNATIONAL CONSIGNMENT NOTE

1 Sender (name, address, country) Expediteur (nom, adresse, pays)	2/3 Sender's/agent's reference Reference de l'expediteur/de l'agent
4 Consignee (name, address, country) Destination (nom, adresse, pays)	5 Carrier (name, address, country) Transporteur (nom, adresse, pays)
6 Place & date of taking over the goods (place, country, date) / Lieu et date de la prise en charge des marchandises (lieu, pays, date)	7 Succesive carriers Transporteurs successifs
8 Place designated for delivery of goods (place, country) / Lieu prevu pour la livraison des marchandises (lieu, pays)	This carriage is subject, notwithstanding any clause to the contrary, to the Convention on the Contract for the International Carriage of Goods by Road (CMR). Ce transport est soumis nonobstant toute clause contraire a la Convention Relative au Contratde Transport International de Marchandises par Route (CMR)

9 Shipping marks; no. & kind of packages; description of goods * Marques et nos; no et nature des colis; designation des marchandises*	10 Gross weight (kg) Poids brut (kg)	11 Volume (m3) Cubage (m3)

12 Carriage charges Prix de transport	13 Senders instructions for customs, etc... Instructions de l'expediteur (optional)

14 Reservations Reserves	15 Documents attached Documents annexes (optional)
	16 Special agreements Conventions particulieres (optional)

17 Goods received Marchandises recues	18 Signature of carrier Signature du transporteur	19 Company completing this note Societe emettrice
		20 Place and date; signature Lieu et date; signature

COPY 1 SENDER
COPY 2 CONSIGNEE
COPY 3 CARRIER

Approved by FTA/RHA/SITPRO UK 1981/1987/1993
*NB FOR DANGEROUS GOODS SPECIFY: 1. Substance identification number (if applicable) 2. Substance description 3. Class 4. Item number and letter (if any) 5. The initials "ADR" or "RID" 6. Other statements as required by ADR or RID.

PHOTOCOPIABLE FORMS

BILL OF LADING FOR COMBINED TRANSPORT SHIPMENT OR PORT TO PORT SHIPMENT B/L No.:

Shipper	Reference:
Consigned to the order of	**P&O Containers**
Notify Party/Address (It is agreed that no responsibility shall attach to the Carrier or his Agents for failure to notify of the arrival of the goods (see clause 20 on reverse))	Place of Receipt (Applicable only when this document is used as a Combined Transport Bill of Lading)
Pre-Carrier	Place of Delivery (Applicable only when this document is used as a Combined Transport Bill of Lading)
Vessel and Voy. No.	
Port of Loading	Port of Discharge	

Undermentioned particulars as declared by Shipper, but not acknowledged by the Carrier (see Clause 11)

Marks and Nos; Container Nos;	Number and kind of Packages; Description of Goods	Gross Weight (kg)	Measurement (cbm)

*Total No. of Containers/Packages received by the Carrier	Movement	Freight payable at

Received by the Carrier from the Shipper in apparent good order and condition (unless otherwise noted herein) the total number or quantity of Containers or other packages or units indicated in the box above entitled "*Total No. of Containers/Packages received by the Carrier" for Carriage subject to all the terms and conditions hereof (INCLUDING THE TERMS AND CONDITIONS ON THE REVERSE HEREOF AND THE TERMS AND CONDITIONS OF THE CARRIER'S APPLICABLE TARIFF) from the Place of Receipt or the Port of Loading, whichever is applicable, to the Port of Discharge or the Place of Delivery, whichever is applicable. Before the Carrier arranges delivery of the Goods one original Bill of Lading, duly endorsed, must be surrendered by the Merchant to the Carrier at the Port of Discharge or at some other location acceptable to the Carrier. In accepting this Bill of Lading the Merchant expressly accepts and agrees to all its terms and conditions whether printed, stamped or written, or otherwise incorporated, notwithstanding the non-signing of this Bill of Lading by the Merchant.

Number of Original Bills of Lading	Place and Date of Issue	IN WITNESS of the contract herein contained the number of originals stated opposite has been issued, one of which being accomplished the other(s) to be void.

P&O Containers Ltd, 70469 Stuttgart

125		7463 8616				CSR/EC1				125-7463 8616	
Shipper's Name and Address		Shipper's Account Number				Not negotiable **Air Waybill** Issued by British Airways London Member of IATA				**BRITISH AIRWAYS** ***WORLD CARGO***	
						Copies 1, 2 and 3 of this Air Waybill are originals and have the same validity					
Consignee's Name and Address		Consignee's Account Number				It is agreed that the goods described herein are accepted in apparent good order and condition (except as noted) for carriage SUBJECT TO THE CONDITIONS OF CONTRACT ON THE REVERSE HEREOF. ALL GOODS MAY BE CARRIED BY ANY OTHER MEANS INCLUDING ROAD OR ANY OTHER CARRIER UNLESS SPECIFIC CONTRARY INSTRUCTIONS ARE GIVEN HEREON BY THE SHIPPER, AND SHIPPER AGREES THAT THE SHIPMENT MAY BE CARRIED VIA INTERMEDIATE STOPPING PLACES WHICH THE CARRIER DEEMS APPROPRIATE. THE SHIPPER'S ATTENTION IS DRAWN TO THE NOTICE CONCERNING CARRIER'S LIMITATION OF LIABILITY. Shipper may increase such limitation of liability by declaring a higher value for carriage and paying a supplemental charge if required.					
Telephone Number						ISSUING CARRIER MAINTAINS CARGO ACCIDENT LIABILITY INSURANCE					
Issuing Carrier's Agent Name and City						Accounting Information					
Agent's IATA Code		Account No.									
Airport of Departure (Addr. of First Carrier) and Requested Routing											
To	By First Carrier	Routing and Destination	to	by	to	by	Currency	CHGS Code	WT/VAL PPD COLL	Other PPD COLL	Declared Value for Carriage	Declared Value for Customs
Airport of Destination		Flight/Date	For Carrier Use only	Flight/Date							
Handling Information										SCI	

No. of Pieces RCP	Gross Weight	kg lb	Rate Class / Commodity Item No.	Chargeable Weight	Rate / Charge		Total	Nature and Quantity of Goods (incl. Dimensions or Volume)

Prepaid	Weight Charge	Collect	Other Charges
	Valuation Charge		
	Tax		
	Total Other Charges Due Agent		Shipper certifies that the particulars on the face hereof are correct and that **insofar as any part of the consignment contains dangerous goods, such part is properly described by name and is in proper condition for carriage by air according to the applicable Dangerous Goods Regulations.**
	Total Other Charges Due Carrier		
			Signature of Shipper or his Agent
Total Prepaid		Total Collect	
Currency Conversion Rates		CC Charges in Dest. Currency	Executed on (date) at (place) Signature of Issuing Carrier or its Agent
For Carriers Use only at Destination		Charges at Destination	Total Collect Charges 125- 7463 8616

Seller (name, address, VAT reg. no.)

COMMERCIAL INVOICE
for exports to the UNITED STATES OF AMERICA

Invoice number	Seller's U.S. Customs identity code
Invoice date (tax point)	Seller's reference
Buyer's reference	Other reference

Consignee

Buyer (if not consignee)

Transport information

Country of origin of goods

Terms of delivery and payment

Vessel/flight no. and date	Port/airport of loading

Port/airport of discharge	Place of final destination	Currency used	Exchange rate (if fixed or agreed)	Date order accepted

Shipping marks; container number	No. and kind of packages; description of goods	Commodity code	Total gross wt (kg)	Total cube (m³)
			Total net wt (kg)	

Item/packages	Gross/net/cube	Description	Quantity	Unit price		Amount
				Home Market	Invoice	

Enumerate the following charges and state if each amount has been included in the total selling price to purchaser and current domestic values column above.

	Selling price to purchaser		Invoice total
	Amount (state currency)	State if included	
1. Value of outside packages/containers			
2. Labour in packing goods into outside packages/containers			
3. Inland transport and insurance charges to dock/airport area			
4. Dock and port charges			
5. Overseas freight			
6. Overseas insurance			
7. Details of any other charges relating to delivery of goods			
8. Rebates, drawbacks and discounts (state full particulars)			

EXPORTER'S DECLARATION
It is hereby certified that this invoice shows the actual price of the goods described, that no other invoice has been or will be issued, and that all particulars are true and correct.

Name of signatory

Place and date of issue

Signature

NIGERIA
CERTIFICATE OF VALUE

Form C 16

*) **I,** _____
of _____

**) Manufacturer/Supplier/Exporter of the goods enumerated in this invoice amounting to _____

hereby declare that I have the authority to make and sign this certificate on behalf of the aforesaid **)Manufacturer/Supplier/Exporter and that I have the means of knowing and I do hereby certify as follows:—

(1) That this invoice is in all respects correct and contains a true and full statement of the price actually paid or to be paid for the said goods, and the actual quantity thereof.

(2) That no different invoice of the goods mentioned in the said invoice has been or will be furnished to anyone.

(3) That no arrangement or understanding affecting the purchase price of the said goods has been or will be made or entered into between the said exporter and purchaser or by anyone on behalf of either of them either by way of discount, rebate, compensation or in any manner whatever other than as fully shown on this invoice.

DATED at _____ this _____ day of _____

_____ _____
(Signature of Witness) (Signature)

CERTIFICATE OF ORIGIN

*) **I,** _____
of _____

**) Manufacturer/Supplier/Exporter of the goods enumerated in this invoice hereby declare that I have the authority to make and sign this certificate on behalf of the aforesaid **) Manufacturer/Supplier/Exporter and that I have the means of knowing and I do hereby certify as follows:—

(1) That all the goods mentioned in this invoice have been wholly produced or manufactured

in _____

(2) That all the goods mentioned in this invoice have been either wholly or partially produced or manufactured

in _____

(3) That as regards those goods only partially produced or manufactured,

(a) the final process or processes of manufacture have been performed in _____

(b) the expenditure in material produced and/or labour performed in _____ calculated subject to qualifications hereunder, in the case of all such goods is not less than 25 per cent of the factory or works costs of all such goods in their finished state. (See note below)

(4) That in the calculation of such proportion of material produced and/or labour performed none of the following items has been included or considered:—
Manufacturer's profit, or remuneration of any trader, agent, broker or other person dealing in the goods in their finished condition; royalties; cost of outside packages, or any cost of packing the goods thereinto; any cost of conveying, insuring, or shipping the goods subsequent to their manufacture.

DATED at _____ this _____ day of _____

_____ _____
(Signature of Witness) (Signature)

Note:
* (1) The person making the declaration should be a principal or a manager, chief clerk, secretary, or responsible employee.
  (2) The place or country of origin of imports is that in which the goods were produced or manufactured and, in the case of partly manufactured goods, the place or country in which any final operation, has altered to any appreciable extent the character, composition and value of goods imported into that country.
  (3) In the case of goods which have at some stage entered into the commerce of, or undergone a process of manufacture in a foreign country, only that labour and material which are expected on or added to the goods after their return to the exporting territory, shall be regarded as the produce or manufacture of the territory in calculating the proportion of labour and material in the factory or works cost of the finished article.
** (4) Delete the inapplicable.

Enumerate the following charges and state whether each amount has been included in or excluded from the selling price to purchaser:—	Amount in currency of exporting country	State if included in selling price to purchaser
(1) Cost of packing		
(2) Freight		
(3) Insurance		
(4) Commissions (including head office); confirming house and buying commission		
(5) Other charges		

I Industries

1. Primary industries

agriculture *n*	Landwirtschaft
basic materials *npl*	Grundstoffe
cattle raising *n*	Viehzucht
farming *n*	Landwirtschaft

Agricultural machinery has changed farming from a labo(u)r-intensive industry to a capital-intensive industrie.

Der landwirtschaftliche Maschinenpark hat die Landwirtschaft von einer arbeitsintensiven zu einer kapitalintensiven Industrie gemacht.

fishery *n* — Fischerei
forestry *n* — Forstwirtschaft

Forestry is the science of developing and cultivating forests.

Forstwirtschaft ist die Wissenschaft von der Entwicklung und Pflege der Wälder.

mining *n* — Bergbau

Coal mining declined as oil and gas replaced coal as the principal industrial and home heating fuels.

Als Öl und Gas die Kohle als den Hauptbrennstoff in der Industrie und den Privathaushalten ersetzte, ging der Kohlebergbau zurück.

primary *adj* — primär

Primary industries provide basic materials such as wood, coal and farm produce.

Primärindustrien stellen Grundstoffe wie Holz, Kohle und landwirtschaftliche Erzeugnisse bereit.

prospect *v* — nach Bodenschätzen suchen

John moved to Alaska to prospect for gold and silver.

John zog nach Alaska, um dort nach Gold und Silber zu suchen.

quarry *v, n* — Steine brechen, Steine abbauen; Steinbruch

Energy

fossil fuel *n*	fossiler Brennstoff
hydropower *n*	Wasserkraft
nuclear power *n*	Atomkraft
oil rig *n*	Ölbohrinsel, Ölbohrturm
power station *n*, **power plant** *n*	Kraftwerk
power supply *n*	Stromversorgung, Energieversorgung
solar power *n*, **solar energy** *n*	Sonnenenergie, Solarenergie
utility company *n*	Energieunternehmen, Versorgungsunternehmen
wind energy *n*	Windkraft

2. Secondary industries

aerospace *n*	Luft- und Raumfahrt
automobile *n*	Automobil
automotive industry *n*	Automobilindustrie
building *n*	Bau(gewerbe)
capital goods *npl*	Anlagegüter
chemical industry *n*	chemische Industrie
civil engineer *n*	Hoch- und Tiefbauingenieur(in)
clothing industry	Bekleidungsindustrie
consumer goods *npl*	Konsumgüter
electronics *n*	Elektronik
food processing *n*	Nahrungsmittelverarbeitung
heavy industry *n*	Schwerindustrie

Shipbuilding and steel manufacturing are considered heavy industries.

Schiffbau und Stahlherstellung werden zur Schwerindustrie gezählt.

housing *n* — Wohnungen
iron and steel industry *n* — Eisen- und Stahlindustrie
light industry *n* — Leichtindustrie

Light industry manufactures smaller products such as clothing, computers and food products.

Die Leichtindustrie stellt kleinere Produkte her wie z.B. Textilien, Computer und Nahrungsmittelprodukte.

manufacturing *n* — Herstellung, Produktion

Manufacturing is a capital-intensive sector.

Die Güterproduktion ist ein kapitalintensiver Sektor.

mechanical engineering *n* — Maschinenbau

microelectronics *n*	Mikroelektronik
plastics *npl*	Plastikerzeugnisse
precision engineering *n*	Feinmechanik, Präzisionsmechanik
processing *adj*	verarbeitend
Last year was a good one for the processing industry, especially in the plastics and rubber sectors.	Für die verarbeitende Industrie war letztes Jahr ein gutes Jahr, insbesondere für die Kunststoff- und Gummibranche.
producer goods *npl*	Produktionsgüter
Producer goods, such as semi-finished products and machinery, are used to make consumer goods.	Produktionsgüter, wie beispielsweise Halberzeugnisse und Maschinen, werden zur Herstellung von Konsumgütern verwendet.
secondary *adj*	sekundär
Secondary industries use basic raw materials to make manufactured goods.	Sekundärindustrien nutzen Grund- und Rohstoffe zur Herstellung von Industriewaren.
shipbuilding *n*	Schiffbau
steel manufacturing *n*	Stahlherstellung
structural engineer *n*	Ingenieur(in) für (Hoch)bautechnik
textiles *npl*	Textilien; Stoffe

3. Tertiary industries

advertising *n*	Werbung
banking *n*	Bankgeschäft, Bankgewerbe
catering *n*	Gastronomie
The airport catering service supplies warm and cold meals and beverages to aircraft before their departure.	Die Flughafengastronomie liefert vor dem Abflug warme und kalte Speisen und Getränke an das Flugzeug.
commerce *n*	(Binnen- und Außen)handel, Handelsverkehr
communications *npl*	Kommunikation
consultant *n*	Berater(in)
entertainment industry *n*	Unterhaltungsindustrie
export *adj*	Export-
Most of our machinery is sold on export markets.	Die meisten unserer Maschinen werden auf den Exportmärkten verkauft.
film industry *n*	Filmindustrie
foreign *adj*	Auslands-
health care *n*	Gesundheitsfürsorge
home *adj*	Binnen-, Inlands-
Although we are a Canadia company, home market sales only account for 20% of all the whiskey we make; export markets take the rest.	Obwohl wir ein kanadisches Unternehmen sind, macht der Inlandsabsatz nur 20% der gesamten Whiskymenge aus, die wir herstellen. Der Rest geht in den Export.
import *adj*	Import-
The Craig Co. is an import specialist for foreign electronics.	Die Craig Co. ist ein spezialisierter Importeur für ausländische Elektronikerzeugnisse.
insurance *n*	Versicherung
personal services *npl*	persönliche Dienstleistung
publishing *n*	Verlagswesen
service sector *n*	Dienstleistungssektor
tertiary *adj*	tertiär
The tertiary sector of the economy provides services to industry and consumers.	Der tertiäre Sektor der Wirtschaft offeriert der Industrie und den Verbrauchern Dienstleistungen.
tourism *n*	Tourismus
trade *n*	Handel, Gewerbe
transport *n (GB)*; **transportation** *n (US)*	Transport
travel agency *n*	Reisebüro

II Production

1. Works/Plants

assembly plant n	Montagewerk, Fertigungswerk
business park n	Gewerbegebiet, Gewerbepark
close down v, **shut down** v	schließen, zumachen
closure n	Schließung
completion n	Beendigung, Fertigstellung
facilities npl	Betrieb(sstätte)
factory n	Fabrik
factory floor n	Fabrik, Produktionsstätte
floor space n	Grundfläche, Bodenfläche
gate n	Tor
green-field site n (GB)	Grundstück/Standort/Industriegelände auf der grünen Wiese
industrial estate n (GB); **industrial park** n (US)	Gewerbegebiet
industrial site n	Industriegelände
layout n	Gestaltung, Anordnung, Aufteilung, Plan
location n	Standort
plant n	Fabrikationsanlage, Werk
premises npl	Geschäftsräume
purpose-designed adj	speziell entworfen
shop n	Werkstatt, Betrieb, Halle
shop floor n	Fabrik, Werkstatt, Produktionsstätte, Betrieb
works npl	Betrieb, Werk, Fabrik

2. Machinery/Setting-ups

assembly line n	Fließband
conveyor belt n	Förderband, Transportband
gauge n	Messgerät, Messinstrument
gear n	Gang, Getriebe, Zahnrad
machine shop n	(Maschinen)werkstatt, Maschinenhalle
machine tool n	Werkzeugmaschine
maintenance n	Wartung
materials handling n	Materialtransport, innerbetriebliches Transport- und Lagerwesen
power tool n	Elektrowerkzeug
systems engineering n	Anlagenbau, Anlagentechnik
tool n	Werkzeug
tooling n	Werkzeugbestückung, Maschinenausrüstung

3. Automation

CNC machine n	CNC-Maschine (freiprogrammierbare, durch Zahlencode rechnergesteuerte Werkzeugmaschine)
computer-aided manufacturing (CAM) n	computergestützte Fertigung (computergestützte Steuerung und Überwachung der Produktion)
computer-integrated manufacturing (CIM) n Computer integrated manufacturing uses computers to control the complete manufacturing cycle including design, planning and manufacturing.	computerintegrierte Fertigung In der computerintegrierten Fertigung werden Computer benutzt, um den kompletten Fertigungskreislauf einschließlich des Designs, der Planung und der Herstellung zu kontrollieren.
computerization n	Computerisierung
robotics n	Handhabungstechnik, Robotik (Bewegung von Arbeitsstücken durch Roboter)
robotization n	Ausstattung mit Robotern, Robotersteuerung

4. Production/Installation

assemble v
The plant will be assembled and erected on site, with Chinese workers and technicians carrying out all of the work.
bottleneck n
capital-intensive adj
downtime n
efficiency n
erect v
hold-up n
idle adj
labo(u)r-intensive adj
man-hour n
on site adv
overcapacity n
processing n
production line n
production run n
set up v
surplus capacity n, **excess capacity** n
workpiece n

zusammenbauen, montieren
Das Werk wird vor Ort montiert und aufgebaut, wobei chinesische Arbeiter und Techniker die gesamten Arbeiten ausführen.
Engpass
kapitalintensiv
Ausfallzeit
Leistungsfähigkeit
errichten, aufbauen
Verzögerung
frei, ungenutzt, brachliegend
arbeitsintensiv
Arbeitsstunde
vor Ort
Überkapazität
Verarbeitung
Fertigungsstraße, Fließband
Produktionsserie
aufbauen, montieren, zusammenbauen
Überkapazität
Werkstück, Arbeitsstück

5. Production Planning

dismantle v
feasability study n
manufacturing costs npl
outsourcing n

phase in v
phase out v
retooling n
scrap v
speed up v
step up v
streamline v
tool up v
unit cost n

zerlegen, abbauen
Machbarkeitsstudie, Wirtschaftlichkeitsberechnung
Herstellungskosten
Produktionsverlagerung an Subunternehmer, Arbeitsauslagerung
(schrittweise) einführen
(schrittweise) zu Ende gehen lassen
Neuausrüstung, Maschinenerneuerung
verschrotten
beschleunigen, erhöhen
steigern, intensivieren, erhöhen
rationalisieren
maschinell ausstatten, umrüsten
Stückkosten

6. Quality Control

check v
detect v
ensure v (GB); **insure** v (US)
grade n
inspection n
meticulous adj
precaution n
quality assurance n
quality control n
The purpose of our quality control program is to inspect each product several times before it leaves the plant to ensure that it meets our company's quality standards before sale to the customer.

random adj
reject v
shoddy adj
spoilage n
standard n
Our products are expected to meet very high standards.
subquality n

(über)prüfen
herausfinden, aufdecken
sicherstellen
(Reinheits)grad
Inspektion, Begutachtung, Überprüfung
peinlich genau, penibel
Vorsichtsmaßnahme
Qualitätssicherung
Qualitätskontrolle
Der Zweck unserer Qualitätskontrolle besteht darin, jedes Produkt, bevor es das Werk verlässt, mehrfach zu begutachten um sicherzustellen, dass es die Qualitätsanforderungen unserer Firma erfüllt, bevor es an den Verbraucher verkauft wird.
zufällig, stichprobenartig
zurückweisen
minderwertig, schlampig, schludrig
Ausschuss, Verderb
Standard, Anforderung
Von unseren Produkten wird erwartet, dass sie sehr hohen Anforderungen entsprechen.
minderwertige Qualität

7. Storage/Inventory

buffer stock *n,* **reserve stock** *n*	Mindestbestand
continuous stocktaking *n*	permanente Inventur
depot *n,* **warehouse** *n*	Lagerhaus
forklift truck *n (GB);* **forklift** *n (US)*	Gabelstapler
incoming *adj*	eingehend
inventory *n*	Bestandsaufnahme, Inventur, Lagerbestand
itemize *v*	aufführen, auflisten
outgoing *adj*	abgehend, versandt
reorder level *n*	Meldebestand
stock control *n*	Lager(bestands)kontrolle, Lagerwirtschaft
run out of *v*	knapp werden
stock cover *n*	Mindestdeckungsmenge
stockpile *v*	Vorräte anlegen/halten
stocktaking *n (GB);* **inventory** *n (US)*	Bestandsaufnahme, Inventur
stock-in-trade *n*	Warenbestand, Warenvorrat
storage *n*	Lagerung, Lagerhaltung
stores *npl*	Vorräte
warehousing costs *npl*	Lagerkosten
work-in-process *n,* **work in progress** *n*	unfertige Erzeugnisse, laufende Fertigung

III Product

1. General Knowledge

accessory *n*	Zubehör
appliance *n*	Gerät
attachment *n*	Zusatzteil, Zubehörteil
blueprint *n*	Blaupause, Plan, Projektstudie
brand *n*	Marke
brand name *n*	Markenname
by-product *n*	Nebenprodukt, Abfallprodukt
complex *adj*	komplex, differenziert
component *n*	Bauteil
core benefit *n*	Hauptvorteil, Hauptnutzen
core product *n*	wichtigstes Erzeugnis
custom-built *adj*	nach Wunsch des Kunden angefertigt, auf Bestellung
customized *adj*	nach Bestellung gefertigt, nach Wunsch
end user *n*	Endverbraucher(in)
equip *v*	ausrüsten
extra *n*	Extra, Zusatzausstattung
feature *n*	Merkmal, Bestandteil
feature *v*	eine Besonderheit aufweisen
This Suckmore vacuum cleaner features a number of standard attachments and optional accessories that you can use to clean or shampoo carpets or furniture.	Dieser Suckmore Staubsauger weist eine Reihe von besonderen Standardzusatzteilen auf, sowie wahlweise Zubehör, das man benutzen kann, um Teppiche zu säubern oder mit Schaum zu reinigen.
fitting *n*	Montage, Installation, Einbau
fit *v*	einbauen
gadget *n*	Gerät, Vorrichtung, technische Spielerei
general purpose *adj*	universal
install *v*	installieren, einrichten
launch *v, n*	auf den Markt bringen, herausbringen; (Markt)einführung
life cycle *n*	Lebenszyklus
The four stages of a product life cycle are development, growth, maturity and decline.	Die vier Phasen im Lebenszyklus eines Produkts sind Einführung, Wachstum, Reife und Degeneration.
make *n*	Marke, Fabrikat
make up *v*	bestehen aus
Our American television set is mostly made up of components that are imported from Mexico.	Unser amerikanisches Fernsehgerät besteht hauptsächlich aus Bauteilen, die aus Mexiko importiert sind.

maturity *n*	Reife
off-the-shelf *adj*	von der Stange, vorrätig, ab Lager
operate *v*	bedienen
operational *adj*	funktionsfähig, betriebsbereit
optional *adj*	wahlweise, auf Wunsch erhältlich
product life cycle *n*	Produktlebenszyklus
The product life cycle for our automobiles, i.e. the period of time from a car's development to its discontinuation, is generally seven years.	Der Produktlebenszyklus unserer Automobile, d.h. die Zeitspanne von der Entwicklung eines Autos bis zur Produktionseinstellung, beträgt im allgemeinen sieben Jahre.
registered trademark *n*	Warenzeichen
sophisticated *adj*	hochentwickelt, raffiniert
spare *n*, spare part *n*	Ersatzteil
spin-off *n*	Nebenprodukt, Nebeneffekt
tailor-made *adj*	maßgeschneidert
trademark *n*	Handelsmarke, Warenzeichen
winner *n*	Verkaufsschlager
Our sales figures show that our new series of low-priced laser printers is a real winner on the market.	Unsere Verkaufszahlen zeigen, dass unsere neue Baureihe preisgünstiger Laserdrucker ein richtiger Verkaufsschlager auf dem Markt ist.

2. Different Products

basic foodstuffs *npl*	Grundnahrungsmittel
brown goods *npl (GB)*; electronic items *npl (US)*	braune Ware, Unterhaltungselektronik
clothing *n*	Bekleidung
confectionery *n (GB)*; candy *n (US)*	Süßwaren; Konfekt
consumer durables *npl*	langlebige Konsumgüter
cosmetics *npl*	Kosmetikartikel
do-it-yourself *adj*	Do-it-yourself, Heimwerker-
dry goods *npl*	Textilwaren
durable *adj*	langlebig
electrical goods *npl*	Elektroartikel
fancy goods *npl (GB)*; novelty items *npl (US)*	Neuheiten
farm produce *n*	landwirtschaftliches Produkt, Agrarerzeugnis
finished goods *npl*	Fertigwaren, Fertigerzeugnisse
foodstuffs *npl*	Nahrungsmittel
footwear *n*	Schuhwerk
fresh foods *npl*	Frischwaren
frozen foods *npl*	Gefrierkost
hardware *n*	Eisen- und Haushaltswaren
household goods *npl*	Haushaltswaren
jewellery *n (GB)*; jewelry *n (US)*	Schmuck
luxury goods *npl*	Luxusartikel
manufactures *npl*	Industrieprodukte, Industriewaren
manufactured goods *npl*	Industriewaren, Industriegüter
non-durable *adj*	kurzlebig
non-food *adj*	Non-food
Supermarkets also sell non-food items such as light bulbs and magazines.	Supermärkte verkaufen auch Nonfood-Artikel wie z.B. Glühbirnen und Zeitschriften.
semi-finished goods *npl*	Halbfertigwaren, Halberzeugnisse
tinned *adj (GB)*; canned *adj (US)*	in Dosen
toiletries *npl*	Toilettenartikel
white goods *npl*	weiße Ware, Haushaltsgeräte

3. Product Range

assortment *n*	Sortiment, Auswahl, Zusammenstellung
be out of *v*	ausverkauft sein
brand *n*	Sorte
class of products *n*	Warengruppe
clear *v*	räumen, ausverkaufen
Mega Byte Inc. is having a spring computer sale to clear stocks of items that have been discontinued by the manufacturer.	Die Mega Byte Inc. macht einen Frühjahrs-Computerausverkauf, um das Lager von denjenigen Artikeln zu räumen, die vom Hersteller nicht mehr gebaut werden.

comprehensive *adj*	umfassend, weitgespannt
discontinue *v*	einstellen, nicht mehr herstellen, auslaufen lassen, herausnehmen
fast-selling *adj*	gutgehend, umsatzstark, leicht verkäuflich
item *n*	Artikel
keep pace with *phrase*	Schritt halten mit
lay in *v*	(ein)lagern
leader *n*	Spitzenreiter, führender Artikel
overstock *v*	sich überreichlich eindecken, zu große Warenvorräte haben, zu viel auf Lager haben
product line *n*, **line** *n*	Produktlinie
Power tools are one of our company's most important product lines.	Elektrowerkzeuge sind eine der wichtigsten Produktlinien unseres Unternehmens.
product portfolio *n*	Produktpalette
product range *n*	Sortiment
range of goods *n*	Warensortiment
replenish *v*	ergänzen, wiederauffüllen
The store lost approximately $150,000 in sales revenue because it could not replenish its supply of video games before Christmas.	Das Geschäft machte einen Verlust von ungefähr $150.000 an Verkaufsumsätzen, da es seinen Vorrat an Videospielen vor Weihnachten nicht mehr ergänzen konnte.
selection *n*	Auswahl
seller *n*	gängiger Artikel
shelf warmer *n*	Ladenhüter
wide-ranging *adj*	weitreichend, umfassend, breitgefächert

4. Quality

breakdown *n*	Panne
break down *v*	eine Panne haben
commision *v (GB);* **dedicate** *v (US)*	in Dienst stellen
condition *n*	Zustand
defect *n*	Defekt, Fehler
defective *adj*	fehlerhaft, mangelhaft
failure *n*	Versagen, Störung
fair average quality (faq) *n*	Durchschnittsqualität
We can deliver the goods in fair average quality at a price of £36.60 each.	Wir können die Waren in Durchschnittsqualität zu einem Stückpreis von £36,60 liefern.
finish *n*	Oberflächenbearbeitung, Endbearbeitung, Lack(ierung)
first-class quality *n*	erstklassige Qualität
fix *v*	reparieren, in Ordnung bringen
flaw *n*	Mangel, Fehler, Defekt
flawed *adj*	fehlerhaft
We sent the flawed shipment of shirts from Taiwan back to the manufacturer.	Wir schickten die fehlerhafte Hemdensendung aus Taiwan an den Hersteller zurück.
heavy-duty *adj*	strapazierfähig, Hochleistungs-
high-grade *adj*	hochwertig
The manufacturer in Taiwan could not believe that the shirts were flawed. He claimed that only high-grade cloth and non-fading colors had been used to make the shirts.	Der Hersteller in Taiwan konnte nicht glauben, dass seine Hemden Mängel hatten. Er behauptete, dass nur hochwertiger Stoff und lichtechte Farben für die Produktion der Hemden verwendet worden war.
impair *v*	beeinträchtigen
impairment *n*	Beeinträchtigung, Störung
improper *adj*	unsachgemäß, missbräuchlich, nicht ordnungsgemäß
in order *phrase*	in Ordnung
lightweight *adj*	leicht
mark *n*	Fleck
mediocre *adj*	mittelmäßig, mittlere (r, s)
non-fading *adj*	lichtecht
poor quality *n*	schlechte Qualität
rectify *v*	beheben, in Ordnung bringen
-resistant *adj*	-fest
All our watches are shock-resistant.	All unsere Armbanduhren sind stoßfest.

seconds *npl*
Our down-market retail stores sell factory seconds, i.e., clothing or merchandise with minor flaws.

soiled *adj*
teething problems *npl (GB);* **bugs** *npl (US);* **quirks** *npl (US);* **gremlins** *npl (US)*
The launch of our new sports car will be delayed for six weeks due to teething problems with the transmission.
up to standard *phrase*
I have the feeling that the service we're getting on our car is not quite up to standard.

warranty *n*
wear and tear *n*
The warranty does not cover parts subject to normal wear and tear or improper use.

workmanship *n*

zweite Wahl
Unsere Einzelhandelsgeschäfte der unteren Preisklasse verkaufen Fabrikwaren zweiter Wahl, d.h. Kleidung oder Waren mit kleinen Fehlern.
verschmutzt
Kinderkrankheiten, Anfangsprobleme

Die Markteinführung unseres neuen Sportwagens wird sich aufgrund von Anfangsproblemen mit dem Getriebe um sechs Wochen verschieben.
den Anforderungen genügend
Ich habe das Gefühl, dass die Wartung, die an unserem Auto vorgenommen wird, nicht den Anforderungen genügt.
Garantie
Abnutzung, Verschleiß
Die Garantie erstreckt sich nicht auf Teile, die dem normalen Verschleiß unterworfen sind oder durch unsachgemäßen Gebrauch verursacht wurden.
Verarbeitung

5. Warranties

buy back *v*
The car salesman promised to buy back the car if we were not 100% satisfied.
contract of service *n*, **service contract** *n*
customer satisfaction *n*
expire *v*
The warranties on most cars made in Germany expire after one year.
expiry date *n (GB);* **expiration date** *n (US)*
life-time *adj*
margin of error *n*
sell-by date *n*
Trade Description Act *n (GB)*
unconditional *adj*
use-by date *n*
valid *adj*

zurücknehmen
Der Autoverkäufer versprach, das Auto zurückzunehmen, falls wir nicht 100%ig zufrieden wären.
Wartungsvertrag
Zufriedenheit der Kunden
auslaufen, ablaufen
Die Garantien auf die meisten in Deutschland hergestellten Autos laufen nach einem Jahr ab.
Verfallsdatum, Ablaufdatum, Fälligkeitstermin
Lebenszeit-, lebenslang
Fehlerbereich, Fehlerspielraum
Mindesthaltbarkeitsdatum
Warenkennzeichnungsgesetz
bedingungslos, uneingeschränkt, vorbehaltlos
Mindesthaltbarkeitsdatum
gültig

6. Styling and Characteristics of Products

adjustable *adj*
alter *v*
breakthrough *n*
built-in *adj*
I just bought a new PC with a built-in Pentium processor and an integrated visual display unit.

economical *adj*
environment-friendly *adj*
facility *n*
Our new car features a remote-controlled central locking facility.
fully automatic *adj*
hard-wearing *adj*
high-end *adj (GB);* **top of the line** *adj (US)*
high-performance *adj*
housing *n*
integrated *adj*
kit *n*

verstellbar
ändern
Durchbruch
eingebaut, Einbau-
Ich habe soeben einen neuen PC mit eingebautem Pentium-Prozessor und integriertem Bildschirm gekauft.
sparsam
umweltfreundlich
Einrichtung, Anlage
Unser neues Auto verfügt über eine fernbedienbare Zentralverriegelungseinrichtung.
vollautomatisch
strapazierfähig, verschleißfest
Spitzen-
Hochleistungs-
Gehäuse
integriert
Bausatz

knock-down *adj*	zerlegt
We have decided to export knock-down machines to Indonesia and have our engineers assemble them there.	Wir haben beschlossen, zerlegte Maschinen nach Indonesien zu senden und sie dort von unseren Ingenieuren zusammenbauen zu lassen.
module *n*	Modul
obsolete *adj*	veraltet
one-touch *adj*	Berührungs-, Sensor-
The assembly line is equipped with a one-touch, push-button stop switch that will shut down operations in case of an emergency or a malfunction.	Das Fließband ist mit einem Sensortastenausschalter ausgestattet, mit dem man im Notfall oder bei einer Fehlfunktion den Betrieb ausschaltet.
out of date *adj*, **outdated** *adj*	veraltet, unzeitgemäß
performance *n*	Leistung
powered *adj*	angetrieben
Uncle Bob bought a new solar-powered calculator.	Onkel Bob hat einen neuen Solarrechner gekauft.
push-botton *adj*	Tasten-
redesign *v*	umgestalten
remote-controlled *adj*	ferngesteuert
replace *v*	ersetzen
reposition *v*	verlagern
revamp *v*	aufpolieren, neu gestalten, modernisieren
shelf-life *n*	Haltbarkeit
Canned foods usually have a longer shelf-life than frozen foods.	Lebensmittelkonserven sind normalerweise länger haltbar als Gefrierkost.
state-of-the-art *adj*	auf dem neuesten Stand der Technik
styling *n*	Gestaltung, Formgebung, Styling, Design
substitute *v*	ersetzen
supersede *v*	ablösen, ersetzen, an die Stelle treten
trial *adj*	Versuchs-, Probe-, Test-
After our first prototype car exploded during a trial run, our engineers modified the fuel system.	Nachdem unser erster Prototyp des Autos während eines Probelaufs explodierte, modifizierten unsere Ingenieure das Treibstoffsystem.
update *v*	auf den neusten Stand bringen
user-friendly *adj*	anwenderfreundlich, benutzerfreundlich
variant *n*	Variante

7. Packing

airtight *adj*	luftdicht
bag *n*	Beutel, Sack, Tüte
bale *n*	Ballen
barrel *n*	Barrel, Fass
batten *v*	mit Latten verstärken
bolt *v*	mit Bolzen befestigen
brace *n*	Strebe, Verstrebung
bubble pack *n*, **blister pack** *n*	Klarsichtpackung
canvas *n*	Segeltuch
carboy *n*	Korbflasche
carton *n*	Karton
case *n*	Kiste
caution marks *npl*	Sicherheitsmarkierungen
cleat *v*	mit Querleisten versehen
crate *n*	(Latten)kiste
drum *n*	Tonne
empties *npl*	Leergut
insulated *adj*	isoliert
lined *adj*	ausgekleidet, gefüttert
packing *n*	Verpacken, Verpackung
padding *n*	Polsterung, Polstermaterial, Füllmaterial
pallet *n*	Palette
sealed *adj*	versiegelt
waterproof *adj*	wasserdicht
wrapping *n*	(Einwickel)verpackung

(from: Thematischer Wirtschaftswortschatz Englisch. Ernst Klett Verlag GmbH, Stuttgart 1995)